MOVEMENT FOR PERIOD PLAYS

by
Bari Rolfe

Cover and Illustrations
by Terry Clark

PERSONABOOKS
1985

CONTENTS

ACKNOWLEDGEMENTS

I owe by far the most thanks to Trish Arnold, trusted colleague, who has been a valued friend and supportive critic through years of stimulating professional discussion and exchange. From her many years at the London Academy of Music and Dramatic Art, she taught me much of what I know about period movement; she was then generous enough to read the manuscript with her unfailing critical friendly eye. Many improvements are due to her, and any remaining faults are my own.

To other colleagues who were good enough to offer valuable comments, my thanks to Jennifer Martin, Judith Pratt, Susannah Berryman, and Bettye Stratton.

I am indebted to the teaching of Jacques Lecoq for my understanding and use of the mask, the chorus, and the value of silent scenes.

For permission to reprint, I am happy to thank Mr. Merlin Holland for the use of Act II of the 4-act version of *The Importance of Being Earnest* by Oscar Wilde.

The word "actor" is used generically
for both women and men.

PREFACE

The movement aspect of rehearsing for period scenes or plays, in the United States, has tended to limp along behind the work on text. Not for lack of interest in the material, for teachers and directors are well aware of its value, and they also know that experience and training in past periods will help actors to play in all periods, but because of a comparative lack of material in practical, usable form.

Although the needed information on movement and manners is available, it is scattered among the various disciplines of history, costumes, theatre, dance, music, customs, and aesthetics. Few directors or teachers have the time to research out everything they want and bring it together; a production budget may or may not include the services of a choreographer, weapons master, or "movement person." Most reference works, even ones as detailed as Wildeblood and Brinson's *The Polite World*, specialize in only some aspects of movement. Oxenford's *Playing Period Plays*, the most oriented to practical use, is still a reference rather than a workbook.

For these reasons the present volume, which is intended for the acting teacher or director, proposes to try to fill the need for a composite source for rehearsal or class use, with practical exercises. Out of the mass of material available I have selected what would be most useful to actors, but I have not tried to say everything or to cover every contingency. For more details, readers can consult the bibliography for additional sources on history, arts, culture, customs, beliefs and superstitions, dance, weaponry, etc. The bibliography is keyed to periods, and also indexed by subject.

This workbook, briefly summarized, deals with period movement as it concerns the actor; that is, with clothing and its effect on movement and gesture; with appropriate deportment; with bows and curtsies, when and how. It offers the basic steps of dances; for a production it would probably be advisable to bring in a choreographer. These are movements a character would have learned as a young person in that time. Doing the basic dance steps will help the actor find the feel of the period, played either neutral or as a character, or while improvising dialogue. These basic dance steps can be done to music or simply to a drum beat. Improvisations are suggested, consisting of casual exchange in ordinary situations. Appendix A is a list of suggested rehearsal costumes. Appendix B, optional, is a videotape showing basic dance steps and salutations. In scope, it encompasses periods from antiquity to World War I. The material is arranged chronologically and can be offered that way. However, each period is also complete in itself, and can be taken separately or in any sequence. I hope that a certain amount of necessary repetition will be excused on those grounds.

THE LOST TWINS, A MULTI-PERIOD PIECE is a composite play that can be used as a kind of summary of work on various periods. It is based on the familiar theme of lost and reunited twins as it was dramatized by playwrights at different times, from Greece to the present. Act I: Plautus, *The Menachmi* (Roman). Act II: Shakespeare, *Comedy of Errors* (Elizabethan). Act III: Regnard, *Les Jumeaux* (*The Twins*) (Restoration). Act IV: Wilde, *The Importance of Being Earnest*—a scene of mistaken identity (Victorian). Act V: Recognition Scene (contemporary). Another appropriate choice for the final act would be the last scene from *The Boys From Syracuse* but reprint rights were unavailable for this workbook. The final act is placed in modern times so as to offer a useful contrast to the preceding four periods. The whole should be a useful classroom exercise and, I hope, a bit of fun.

In period work the question of authenticity must always be dealt with in one way or another. It would be both impossible and undesirable to attempt a museum copy of something that was done in the past. In Moliere's own day his *Bourgeois Gentilhomme* was played as a ballet of six entrees accompanied by a play, the play itself being secondary to the dancing, music, and Turkish extravaganza which were really the *raison d'être* for the comedy. The staging of a Restoration opera amounted to elaborate movements of machinery interspersed with arias and dances, the drama being casually recited while the noble audience talked, played cards, or took refreshments. George Steiner, in "Shakespeare's Four Hundredth," (*Language and Silence*) points out that Shakespeare used an alphabet that we have largely lost, that our literacy is out of touch with the verbal consciousness, habits of feeling, and reference implicit in an Elizabethan text. This workbook, then, simply offers immersion in the period, which cannot help but affect the scene or rehearsal work, to whatever extent is desired.

In books of etiquette and historical dance one often finds conflicting instructions. These differences are due to regional and national variations, varying distances from the center of fashion, and just plain differences of opinion. The disappearing fashion and the incoming fad often co-existed, and there is no homogeneity in any period. In the main I have drawn upon the information found in *The Polite World* by Wildeblood and Brinson; many other texts (see bibliography) were immensely valuable.

TO THE ACTOR

Learning the manners of a period should not result in being mannered, for one learns the code of what was the natural mode of behavior for the class and the time. People in each period took their behavior for granted as the normal, natural way—a way of life, not a way of movement. Etiquette was, and still is, a reflection of one's time and status, and expresses the relationships between classes and people.

Actors will find it enormously helpful to rehearse always in appropriate costume or some approximation of it, and to keep in mind the relevant image, which would extend also to hair styles. If Ophelia should rehearse in jeans, with thumbs hooked into pants pockets, that won't help her to get away from contemporary stance and movement patterns. The initial suggested exercise in each period, that of miming getting dressed in the clothing of the time, can be used as a warm-up for each session. It is well to remember that clothing reveals the relationships of people to society and to each other, what kind of lives they lead, and how they move.

Only the basic steps are given for the dances; they are an effective exercise since they involve carriage, bearing, and a sense of the form and movement, without the actors needing to be concerned with text or dramatic situation. All references to ballet positions for salutations and dance steps should be taken to mean only a 45° turn-out.

1st
position

2nd
position

3rd
position

4th
position

5th
position

The settings for improvisations are those of ordinary social situations. Although the emphasis is on movement, the situations may permit of a minimal exchange of small talk which can help actors to coordinate unfamiliar speech patterns and unfamiliar movement. Actors are urged to keep dialogue to a minimum because, in the words of one surprised student, "that lets you really focus on the physical part!" In the improvisations actors do not attempt to play characters, but neutral persons in period, allowing them to concentrate on movement in the clothing and on the standard elements of etiquette as they might have been taught to the society at the time. Characterization would, of course, modify all actions; therefore the very same circumstances can also be used to play in character in connection with a given production or scene work.

In approaching period work, young actors today should be aware of three deep-lying elements that to a certain extent are foreign to contemporary American society.

One: Because the gulf between classes was enormous, those born to be served took it very much for granted. The upper classes—and it is they who largely populate the plays—learned an elaborate system of etiquette and took seriously the task of filling leisure time gracefully. Etiquette was most precise on what passed between one's betters, one's peers, and one's inferiors. At the same time, *noblesse oblige* also entailed responsibilities for less fortunate persons. Servants and tradespeople did not engage in the same kind of sharply defined social exchange, and their movement and gesture would be influenced only by their simpler clothing, their education if any, status, and circumstances.

Two: Clothes were hampering, and they obviously permitted of no manual labor. Clothing was heavy, binding, or cumbersome. No period since classical Greece offered the comfortable dress permitting all movement and easy lounging as do our garments today.

Three: Men looked after women of their class to a much greater degree than is now the case. Men rose when women entered the room, or approached; they conducted, accompanied, protected, and served them. These were the outer good manners.

In general, the dramatic literature of society reflects its value systems, including attitudes toward women, workers, and races. Actors today, even while personally retaining more sensitive awareness, are to find ways to understand those value systems and deal with them in their characters' terms.

A special note to women playing a role in a male disguise. When the plays were written, a woman wearing trousers had a certain piquancy, for player and audience alike, because women until the mid-1960s habitually wore skirts rather than trousers. So Rosalind today has to be aware that pants are in fact a disguise and not an everyday garment.

A suggestion for actors who find it difficult to go beyond a kind of contemporary, naturalistic intimacy, which does not allow for the larger dimension of tragedy, or even of theatre, to emerge. To counteract this, actors can run portions of scenes in slow motion, which tends to eliminate unnecessary motions. They can also rehearse scenes while remaining some distance apart; and rehearsal costumes and props will help.

Iacchus high in glory, thou whose day
Of all is merriest, hither, help our play;
Show, as we throne thee at thy Maiden's side,
How light to thee are our long leagues of way.
Iacchus, happy dancer, be our guide . . .

Aristophanes, "The Happy Dancer"

GREEK/ROMAN

500 BC - 100 BC

THE TIMES – GREECE

The glory that was Greece was founded in part on the great spirit of inquiry that pervaded the time and the people. Large questions occupied the best minds—questions of philosophy, religion, medicine, mathematics, astronomy; in fact, nearly all the sciences were rooted in that time, and Greece also led the world in arts and literature.

The various Greek city-states were democratic in form. That is, democracy was extended to free adult males, usually of wealthy families, but excluded women, slaves, and most of the common people—a political democracy, not a social one. Most of the work in homes, factories, shops, ports, mines, and farms was done by slaves, non-Greeks or "barbarians" (mainly workers from Asia Minor and the Black Sea region), and some Greek freemen.

Ocean-based commerce was important in their agrarian-trading economy. The Greeks were at home on the sea, and traded to all points in the known world. The sea was their country and their teacher: geography, navigation, ship-building, engineering, harbor-building, coinage, and diplomacy developed and flourished. They exported Greek art, science, customs and ideals throughout the Mediterranean world.

* * *

Free theatre presentations were part of certain religious festivals, to which everyone came; they were occasions for great civic splendor and competition for prizes just as were athletic contests. Tragedies, comedies, and satyr plays for contrast were offered in honor of Dionysus, patron god of theatre. The playing space in the outdoor amphitheatre was called the orchestra from the Greek word for dancing, and its form is believed by some to hark back to the circular threshing floor where the people danced in honor of the same Dionysus, god of wine and fertility. The playing space contained an altar, and behind it was a stage.

The choral aspect of Greek tragedy was important; choral movement ranged from dignified to lively mimetic dance as choristers accompanied the songs. The choral leader did recitative, led songs and dances, and participated in the dialogues.

Actors' training was rigorous, for their voices had to be heard in the immense outdoor presentations; they had also to manage robes, maybe platform shoes, and large masks of the various characters—heroes, kings, gods—as they declaimed, recited, or sang. Only men performed in tragedies; women were dancers and gymnasts, and played in comic mimes, a form of spoken farce sketches. The same actors did not appear in both tragedies and comedies in this presentational theatre form. Usually three actors, with the aid of masks, played all the characters, and members of the chorus were townspeople, or soldiers, or whatever was required for group scenes. A wealthy citizen supplied the money to train the chorus. Actors' clothing was essentially the same as was worn in daily life. A tall staff was associated with seers, priests, heralds, messengers, suppliants, beggars, shepherds, and the old, blind, or wise. Slaves, citizens, and often the playwright acted in the plays. Athenian youth received an education by appearing in choruses, studying music and literature; that meant too that the audiences were knowledgeable and critical. Actors were held in great respect in this important institution, which reflected the religious origins and basis of theatre. In the six-day festival, the first day was devoted to procession, the second to 10 choruses, the third to comic plays, and the next three days to tragedies and satyr pieces.

Playwrights were Aeschylus, Sophocles, Euripides, Aristophanes, Thucydides, Socrates, and Menander. Tragic subjects were based on myth, legend, and heroic themes. In them crime was punished, kindness and understanding were primary virtues, humans were weak but tried to be generous and forgiving, avarice and pomposity were ridiculed. Comedy techniques: political pieces, often mocking individuals by name; use of phalli and obscenities; parodies of tragedies and mythology. Aristophanes' witty, clever comedies were fit companions to the tragedies, in contrast to other small, folksy, domestic comic themes. However, a period of civil and political repression set in with Athens' surrender to Macedonia, followed by a conservative government which did not encourage political commentary in plays.

THE TIMES – ROME

By 200 BC Rome was the dominant power in the Mediterranean world; at its height the Empire encompassed all the lands touching the entire Mediterranean and much of the Black Sea shores.

Republican Rome was for several hundred years a model of honorable, upright, heroic living, austerity and orderliness, dedicated to the welfare of Roman ideals—achieved, to be sure, through wars, conquest, and bloody spectacles. Then it declined and decayed into Imperial Rome, a city "in which everything was for sale." Wealthy, safe, given to extravagant ostentation and elegant, luxurious homes, it left the running of affairs to corrupt politicians, after which its ultimate conquest was inevitable.

* * *

In Rome, as in Athens, dramatic performance was associated with the frequent public holidays and religious festivals. Romans enjoyed legendary and historical drama and light domestic comedies, but were especially fond of the farces which had come from Atella—short playlets, burlesques, pantomimes, vulgar variety shows, with songs, puns, dirty jokes, poisonings, cozenings, and other extravagant events: bright, vigorous, and ingeniously plotted. There are similarities between them and the later Renaissance commedia dell'arte.

Other plays were translated and adapted from Greek drama. Even though translated, the plays retained the Greek names of characters and places, mainly to escape the Roman censors. Playwrights had to avoid political allusion, for society's orderly world did not permit a free stage. Mimes, pantomimes, and farces were all liked, but not as much as chariot races and gladiator combat. In Roman tragedy, the chorus was less formal than on the Greek stage; it usually represented crowds, retinues, and armies of the modern stage.

The Roman theatre was as class conscious and ordered as their society; sections of auditoriums were allotted to segments of the population. All classes came to the free plays, including married women if they were accompanied. The audience was truly a cross section of working class community, farmers, and shopkeepers.

The actors were slaves and citizens, often disreputable and lacking civil rights, in a class with ex-slaves. The mimes particularly brought down upon their licentious offerings the wrath of puritanical elements among the philosophers and the Senate, perhaps partly because women played in them. In the theatre of the public places could be found conjurers, clowns, jugglers, fortune tellers, snake charmers, and singers.

The best-known playwrights were Livius Andronicus, Plautus, Terence, and Naevius.

THE CLOTHING

Greek and Roman clothes consisted mainly of tunics, either short or long, and a draped garment, mantle, shawl or scarf. They were made of wool or linen, hand spun, hand woven, and could be valuable—as the robe filched from his wife by Menaechmus to present to Erotium. Garments were comfortable, permitting of easy movement, and pose no problems for actors' movements. Flat sandals made for casual comfort, and at times cloaks or hats could be worn.

Women wore a long tunic, chiton, of many colors, sometimes girdled up once or twice to create a bloused effect or peplum. A mantle could be draped over it. Female garments could be elaborately trimmed, with embroidery, fringe, or tassels. The rich Roman matron spent much time on toilette and adornment, with beauty treatments, hair treatments, baths, massage, make-up, scents, powders, and jewelry.

Men wore either short or long tunics, also with a draped covering if desired. The Roman toga was white, worn by male citizens only, and the number of purple borders on it proclaimed the status of the wearer. One might carry a staff, which could indicate authority or old age; a tall walking stick was favored by many Athenian citizens. Men wore trimmed beards (less often after Alexander's time) and curled hair.

Both sexes wore perfumes and jewelry: rings, buckles and brooches; women wore bracelets, necklaces, earrings, ankle rings, hair pins in their sometimes padded coiffures; they sometimes wore wigs. In the hair they also wore bands, nets, pearl caps, or tiaras.

Class distinctions were evident in clothing, and slaves and humbler workers wore simpler, practical garments, with no drapery or accessories that might interfere with physical labor.

CUSTOMS AND MANNERS, GREECE

Theirs was a land of exceptional physical beauty, beauty of sea, air, and mountains, and the Greeks were well aware of it, absorbing it with every breath. In Athens, the largest city, life was lived in the streets. Markets, water sources, barber shops—all served as centers of news and gossip for masters and servants milling about on foot, women in litters (by permission, and with servants). Philosophers taught their pupils in groves and porticos. A gregarious people, activity centered around the Agora, to which everyone went each day to keep abreast of things.

Women spent most of their time in the home, men outside of it. The women worked wool, did the spinning, embroidering, and cooking, ran the household with the aid of servants, and had the care and early education of

the children. A girl was brought up to expect the dowried marriage which her parents would arrange for her at about age 15, the man around 30, and thereafter she belonged to her husband. Her home was her castle, where she was respected and obeyed. However, according to some tragic poets, some women lamented their lack of rights.

The cultural events of theatre and Olympic games attracted all the people; the Acropolis in Athens seated 15,000. Women could attend the tragic theatre, a tribute to their intelligence. They probably were veiled and seated in a special place. The Greek upper class standard: to live without working, in order to devote oneself to public service, letters, or philosophy.

Decorum in public was the rule. The hand was not to be drawn from under the upper garment on the street. Personal greetings were easy and unconventional, with no ritual or custom similar to our handshake. But to seal an agreement or a pact, two people clasped hands or wrists.

Slaves might kneel, but only in special circumstances; as a rule they were not servile. A superstition had it that one crossed a threshhold with the right foot, for the left one invited bad luck. At the door to a house one called to be let in. If male strangers were received in the home, the women retired. People ate a light breakfast, then a real breakfast at mid-day; the main meal of the day was dinner, taken after sunset.

CUSTOMS AND MANNERS – ROME

The city of Rome was the center of political, administrative, and social life, and the creator of style and manners. Roman citizenship was highly prized, since there were so many excluded from it. The rich had many slaves; a farmer may have had one or two.

Male children were valued, but female children after the first one were not. All children wore a lucky charm, the boys to age 15 and girls until their marriage. They grew up expecting that girls would marry and boys would follow in the father's profession, perhaps that of farmer, soldier, carpenter, butcher, craftsman, or shopkeeper. So girls were trained to housewifery and boys in physical endurance skills. Upper class children could go to school if the parents wished, or could be educated at home. They studied reading, writing, arithmetic (in Roman numerals and with an abacus!) after which boys might study languages and literature, or plan to enter the only respected profession, that of law, which could lead to politics; they could be apprenticed to a public figure. All in all, education in Rome was exclusively practical, in contrast to the Greek love of philosophy and literature.

Man was the ruler in monogamous marriage, and had the power of life and death, or slavery, over the children. Women led circumscribed lives; they had no rights and could be dealt with as their fathers chose. But they had spirit and at times engaged in activist efforts against certain laws, even successfully. Prostitution was a highly acceptable feature in daily life; many comedies had prostitutes as characters.

The main meal of the day was eaten at mid-day or mid-afternoon. Food was eaten with spoons or with the fingers, so they needed bread, napkins, and sponges. House doors were kept bolted, and guarded by a slave—hence Antipholus of Ephesus cannot get into his own house. Meals could be taken by the men while reclining on couches. Sitting down was not an everday affair; it was a matter of ceremony and dignity involving magistrates, women, judges, and guests.

NOTES ON MASK

In playing comedies of this period, actors encounter no special movement problems; a naturalistic dimension of play usually will suffice, the same dimension appropriate for much of contemporary theatre.

But tragedy on a heroic scale requires that actors play larger than life, appropriate to the themes of the great plays. In this respect, any experience with mask training will be of value. Masks can teach one to be economical, bold, and comfortable with immobility—hence larger than life. Each move is precise, simple, and done with total commitment.

There are two aspects, so to speak, of work with masks. One is from the standpoint of actors, which will be dealt with here, to equip them to reach the heightened dimension of the mask, whether they perform in mask or non-mask plays. The second is the mask as a play production element, which is a choice by a playwright or director.

A full face mask, with no mouth opening, is best for this work. After the early exercises, a half mask covering the upper part of the face might be used for work with text. How does a full face mask help to make the torso and its movements more expressive? With the face hidden and the voice stilled— the two most expressive features among the actor's means—there is only one way for the performer to communicate: through the body and its movements. When those movements are simple and economical, a mask seems to invest the space around it with its presence, to charge the surrounding air with importance; it enlarges the stage presence of the body bearing the mask. This is made even more so by the fact that the entire face and figure must be seen as a unit—a long shot rather than a closeup. Time too is charged; the mask requires a tempo different from that of daily life, and is highly effective with moments of immobility. Generally, movements are slower than in reality; they can also be even faster than reality. Both departures from the norm are well supported by the mask.

The sensitive actor approaches a mask, first by simply looking at it; here the identification with it begins. Grecian figures show actors holding and studying a mask; the tragedian Aesophus is said to have studied his mask for a long time as he prepared for a performance. The Noh actor "looks at the bamboo, becomes the bamboo." Donning the mask, actors remain still for a short time, empty—empty of plans, of habitual movement. They observe themselves in mirrors, letting the identification pervade them, fixing the entire image of mask and body in the eye and in the imagination.

Actors then explore, to find (1) the mask's stance, (2) its walk, (3) a single gesture; they walk, stop, look in another direction, turn the body, and walk—five discrete motions; at all times they refrain from preconceived ideas—not to tell the mask but to "listen" to it. Then actors can try large, single, dramatic gestures: You! Halt! Peace. Away! Oh Zeus! They can go from gesture to gesture with no intervening movement between; this will help the bodies become accustomed to economy of movement.

Actors can also enact a short physical sequence from a play, doing it in slow motion. Slow motion, another exercise for economy, enables one to ascertain what moves are essential. Economy of movement is to be emphasized in these exercises, for it is a main ingredient in playing larger than life, in a tragic dimension. Additional material will be found in my book *Behind the Mask.*

Teachers, directors, and actors may want to consult the few sources dealing with mask work:

Campbell, Louis. "The Personal Neutral Mask." ATA *Theatre News* xi #2, November, 1978.

Eldredge, Sears A. "Jacques Copeau and the Mask in Actor Training." *Mime, Mask & Marionette 2*, nos. 3,4 (1979–80): 187–230.

———— "Masks: Their Use and Effectiveness in Actor Training Programs." Doc. Diss. Michigan State U., 1975.

———— & Hollis Huston. "Actor Training in the Neutral Mask." *TDR XXII*, 4 (T80) Dec. 1978: 19–28.

O'Neill, Eugene. "Memorandum on Masks." *Playwrights on Playwriting*, ed. Toby Cole. NY: Hill & Wang, 1960. Also in *Modern Theatre*, ed. Robert Corrigan. NY: Macmillan, 1964.

Pitt, Leonard. "Mask Technique for the Actor." *San Francisco Theatre I*, 2 (Winter 1977): 81–83.

Rolfe, Bari. *Behind the Mask.* Oakland: Personabooks, 1977.

St. Denis, Michel. *Theatre: The Rediscovery of Style.* NY: Theatre Arts Books, 1960.

Turner, Craig. "Experimenting with Japanese No Masks in Western Actor Training." ATA *Theatre News* xxi, 11 (Nov. 1980).

THE GREEK CHORUS AND ITS MOVEMENTS

Another unfamiliar element in plays of antiquity is the Greek chorus. The tragic chorus comprised 15 people, sometimes divided into two demi-choruses of seven plus a leader. The comic chorus had 24. They represented townsfolk, elders, furies, slaves, mourners, etc., and could be deployed in many different ways.

Because the individuals in a chorus improvise their moves (as in any crowd scene) within given parameters, they must be sensitive to all the others; they fulfill their choral function by thinking and breathing together, and by felt, unsignaled agreements. Jacques Lecoq says that each chorister is $^1/_{15}$th of a chorus of 15. Michael Chekhov comments that the mistake of actors in a crowd scene is that they either try to carry the entire load, or else shift the burden onto all the others. Needed, therefore, is the awareness and sensitivity that enables individuals in a group to give and take, blend, lead and follow, in order to participate in the totality of the choral function.

Exercises based on mutual dependence teach the actor to be "available" to others, to recognize and respond to the stage situation, to trust in spontaneity in the process of molding a group capable of united action and of dynamic variation within the whole. The following exercises are physical in form, to insure that very basic requirement: that actors look at each other. As one surprised student said, "It really makes you pay attention to everyone else!" The exercises are divided into two sections: I Choral Dynamics, and II The Chorus in Action.

I CHORAL DYNAMICS

Some of these suggested exercises will be familiar (who *hasn't* done the mirror!) to some as theatre games, and teachers will have their own favorites. All trust and spontaneity excercises will be useful. The main criterion for including an exercise in this section is that it requires interdependence — that is, an actor's choice of movement is dependent on what another actor does.

1. Mirror exercise in partners, one leading and the other following. Important: the leader is responsible for the follower, must make it easy to follow exactly, at the same time.

1a. With no overt signal, let the leadership change back and forth, whenever it happens. At times the two people may not be sure who is leading.

1b. Place the group in a circle with partners opposite each other. Repeat mirroring. Then let each person mirror anyone they can see, partner or anyone else; this can change as often as desired. There is a tendency for several people to mirror the same person, or their mirror image, and it happens that the entire circle is mirroring itself, everyone doing the same movements, everyone leading and following.

1c. Complementary mirror. Have couples begin the mirror; then, at the option of the follower, instead of copying the movements of the leader, the follower performs complementary ones. These can be: the same movement on a different level, in different time, opposite in time, space, energy, or quality, or . . . . This exercise is especially useful for later choral work, when actors are searching for variations of the same image.

2. Warp and weft. Group lines up by forming two touching sides of a square, the lines at right angle to each other. The two people at the juncture of the angle begin, on hands and knees, to weave—one over, one under. The next persons on each side weave the next threads, and so on. Not too close, and not too fast.

2a. Instead of hands and knees, choose any one of a dozen modes of progressing: slither, hop, roll, etc.

3. Balance for two (or do contact improvisation here). Partners on floor, in any position. Take hold of wrists, or shoulder, or arm, leg, neck, and slowly rise together, the two bodies forming a mass over the common center of balance. Then go back down.

3a. Do with larger groups, three or four persons.

3b. In couples, walk while leaning back to back. Walk with three legs.

4. Equidistance, circle. Everyone in a line, holding hands. The leader will lead the line around to form a circle, defining its perimeter simply by walking it. At the moment that the last in line has reached the perimeter of the circle, everyone drops hands, continues walking. They then adjust the spaces between them, trying to make the intervals equidistant. When all intervals are equal, the group stops at the same moment. In this exercise you are trying to find that one moment of felt agreement—the group fairly breathes together.

5. Equidistance, space. With everyone standing in a bunch, one person steps into the playing area and defines a closed form by walking its outer edge—square or circle or rectangle or . . . . As soon as the form is completed all enter it and keep walking about within the form, trying to stay equal distances from everyone else. There is no built-in finish to this exercise, and a teacher can call out "Freeze!" at times to check out the spacing. One can also direct the group to expand or contract the form while continuously walking, which calls for even more observation and awareness.

6. Machine. Work in groups of about five people. One begins with any simple, machine-like movement. Another person adds a complementary motion, then a third, and so on. Note: avoid simple repetition. Find rhythmic variation. Seek to complicate the workings of the machine, not just add on. Use any and all parts of the body. Have total body identified with machine, even if only an arm or a leg is working.

6a. Two people at a distance from each other each begin their own mechanical movement. The others fill the space between them with parts of the machine, so that the mechanical action begun at one end logically culminates in that of the other end.

6b. Make one enormous machine, the whole group.

6c. Not a machine, but a realistic human action. One person begins an activity—planting, carpentry, sports, etc. Others one by one add a complementary action—that which completes, or adds to, the action and not just a repetition of it. Try to extend, or add detailed depth to, what is already there; not to change the situation but to be sensitive to its possibilities.

II THE CHORUS IN ACTION

A chorus can represent people, animals, objects, elements, attributes, allegorical beings. It breathes, reflects, comments, reacts; it gives birth to its leader, sustains or defends or substitutes for its hero. It can suggest action: fear in the faces of onlookers to an event. It can imitate action: unconscious mimicry by those watching an event. It can be the antagonist: "The Lottery" by Shirley Jackson. It can combine functions. George Kernodle shows in detail how a chorus can mime off-stage violence, can mime not the direct action but a parallel, symbolic one, can enact metaphorically what an actor is experiencing mentally. The purpose of a chorus can be that of non-realistic, symbolic action that can turn an action into myth.

Choristers can enter singly, or in symmetrical ranks, or rush in terrified, or enter silently. The movements should be simple, and exaggerated. The chorus can act as a unit, can divide into groups or individuals with varied reactions. Movements of bacchic chorus can be wild, joyous, drunken, lewd.

A teacher or director should not be intimidated by the question of authenticity, for that is not the purpose of these exercises. Rather they are offered as an indication of the dimension of stance and gesture to be sought for, a dimension commensurate with that of the mask. Here are some conventional gestures for groups to work on, trying for varying degrees of intensity and for variations of a gesture or posture.

Grief, suffering: hands support head; hands raised to forehead; veiling of head or eyes.

Mourning: tear hair, garments, cheeks.

Fear, timidity, shame, sorrow: hang head and look at ground; beat head or breast; run away, tremble.

Supplication: kneel at feet and clasp knees, may add other hand reaching for chin or beard; strike ground rhythmically with hands; standing, eyes heavenward, forearms slightly lifted and palms up.

Prayer: arms stretched heavenward to Olympian gods, palms up; to earthly or demonic beings, palms down and strike ground with foot.

Anxiety, distress: beat head or breast; supplication at altar and touch sacred images; rush about.

Anguish: sink to ground; lie prostrate; pace back and forth.

Perplexity, apprehension: turn away; turn this way and that; peer anxiously.

Hate: gesture of spitting.

Pity: act of assistance.

Joy: cling to another.

Deep sorrow: cries in shrill and in low tones; howling; shrieking.

EXERCISES

Choristers walk about at random, neutral, while instructor keeps time. Instructor calls out an emotion (grief, joy, etc.) and choristers immediately take on an attitude expressive of it, either individually or relating to another. It would be useful to explore various intensities of such attitudes; they will give variety and drama to a group in movement or in tableaux. Then all resume walking until another emotion is called for.

For additional detailed description of conventional choral movement, see Arnott, Kernodle, Lawler.

Jacke took his pype and began to blowe,
Then the friar, as I trowe,
Began to daunce soone,
As soone as he the pype herd,
Like a wood-man he fared,
He lepte and daunced a boute; . . .

Anonymous, "The Dancing Friar"

Medieval/Early Tudor

1200 - 1550

THE TIMES

A certain stasis marked relationships in the Middle Ages. Birth and status governed one's life (said to be true also of angels and birds); everyone knew what to expect, and what was expected of each. Therefore one strove for a state of inner grace, revealed by a heroic and demanding moral code, which would govern one's duty to God, one's lord, the church, and one's peers.

The chivalric code governed the relationships among the upper classes and was taken very seriously, even though the rules were at times broken. The spirit of chivalry called for a knight to honor and cherish the female sex of his class; at the same time some people believed that women did not possess a soul, and women had few or no civil rights. Opinion on whether they should be educated or not was divided. However, mistresses of castles often governed their lands in the absence of their husbands and proved to be formidable adversaries when the need arose.

Great movements of the early Renaissance then shook this static world, movements that fanned out from Italy and affected every aspect of life. A rising merchant class soon rivaled the nobility in power. The age of science opened, printing was invented, the religious reformation began, America was discovered, and national consciousness was growing. Improved navigation led to increased trade, and ideas as well as commodities were exchanged.

* * *

The earlier medieval mystery, miracle, and morality plays were often acted sermons, frequently in dumb show (pantomime) or *tableaux vivants*. Their religious purpose was educative for audiences were largely illiterate. Popular sermons, they gradually included song, music, and drama; they also moved from the church interior to its exterior, then to the marketplace, all the while changing in certain respects. The end of the fifteenth century saw short plays, moral and allegorical, performed in the open or in the great halls, by guilds and municipalities rather than by clerics. Audacious rustic themes were included, which did not help the status of actors, classed as vagabonds, in the eyes of the clergy and civil authorities.

The rhetorical exercises so important in the university curricula helped to pave the way toward the stage as such, and professional groups were attached to the houses of the nobility. There were also pageants, processions, interludes, Robin Hood plays, Sword Plays, Morris Dances—all rather like vaudeville or masque-dialogue. The translating of ancient Greek and Roman playwrights moved the theatre still further from the church.

On the stage (written or set in the period): Morality, cycle plays, commedia dell'arte, Ralph Roister Doister, Pierre Pathelin, Gammer Gurton's Needle, Gorboduc, St. Joan, The Man Who Married a Dumb Wife, Dr. Faustus, The Lady's Not For Burning, Machiavelli, Ruzante.

In the arts: Giotto, Mantegna, Botticelli, da Vinci, Holbein, Bosch, Durer, Michelangelo, Titian, Raphael, Bacon, Dante, Erasmus, Petrarch, Boccaccio, Chaucer, Rabelais.

THE CLOTHING

Clothes were a symbol of status, and sumptuary laws tried to restrict the wearing of ermine, ornaments, jewels, colors, etc. to the class permitted them. The silhouette of the time was the Gothic arch. Clothes, dances, and movement were vertical. Long drapery for men and women, following the lines of the body, were not constricting but were heavy, and governed the rhythms of moving and of the space it filled. Even in sitting, one sat high to be closer to God and angels (dwarfs were therefore closer to the devil!).

Weighty fabrics fell from shoulders and hips, so movements were controlled and large enough to avoid entangling oneself in sleeves or veils. Because of the headgear, the head tended to move with the torso, but not stiffly. Blazonry or family colors were worn on dress, reminding us that it was an illiterate age (serving the same purpose as the Scottish plaid). Shoes and boots were soft, without heels.

Men wore their hair shoulder length. Under robes they wore long hose and soft boots. Women wore their hair loose until marriage. A fashionable lady's gown or surcote trailed both front and back and had to be held up with

one or both hands, or tucked into the girdle, or held close to the body with the forearm. If she walked with the back train trailing, she had to maneuver it by walking around it in order to reverse direction, and to turn in place in order to sit. Everyone wore a purse hanging from the belt or girdle, for there were no pockets.

They could carry gloves, pomanders (apple-shaped caskets containing aromatic substances, "against the plague" or unpleasant odors); men wore daggers; everyone wore cloaks. Jewels were a passion with both sexes—they wore chains to fasten cloaks, jeweled belts, earrings, diadems, clasps, and brooches.

Surviving into the present from this time are the uniforms of the Vatican Swiss Guards (said to have been designed by Michelangelo), the Yeomen of the Guards, the academic gown with mortarboard, and clerical robes.

 The Gothic silhouette changed drastically with the Tudors in the early 16th century, to that of a square. Men's doublets, shortened from the robe, and coats reaching to the thigh matched the shoulders, trousers, and sleeves now bulked out. The women's farthingale pushed skirts out horizontally, and the shoulders too extended out to the sides. Two ladies passing close were like two hay-carts meeting on a path, said a contemporary wit. Boned bodices encased the ribcage, and hoops billowed out the skirts. To manage them, women walked with small, smooth, gliding steps in order to keep the skirt from swaying, and when the wearer stopped the skirt was not to continue to move—all this without using the hands.

NOTE TO STUDENTS: to achieve the above, the body is kept centered over the center of the skirt when coming to a stop. To sit in a farthingale, one approaches a chair and, with a small movement of the hip sweeps half of the skirt past the chair; one then takes a small step back, feeling for the chair with a foot or leg if necessary, and sits. These maneuvers should be unnotice-

 able. Hands can rest gently on the farthingale. Narrow doorways require one to enter sideways—but not crablike—by a light swing to one side, passing through first with one hip, all in one flowing movement as though tracing an S-curve.

Accessories were purses, patches, masks, muffs, veils, sweet box, round fans; indoors perhaps scissors, needlecase, and keys. Items were worn suspended from the waist by a cord.

Expanded trade brought fabrics from all over the known world and men broke out in sartorial display with rings, lace, jeweled belts and buckles. The doublet and hose were set off well by a rather swaggering pose, with feet well apart, especially with the bulky Tudor trousers. Men wore swords, short canes, daggers, mirrors, handkerchiefs, gauntlets or gloves, purses, chains, muffs, and jewelry.

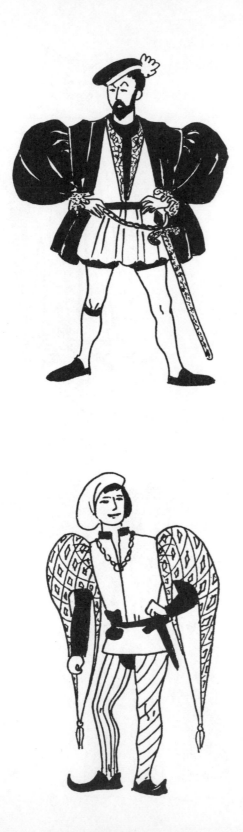

EXERCISES ON DRESS AND MOVEMENT

First, examine the drawings of the clothing; also look at costume books in the library (see the bibliography and/or your own library). Choose a picture and, working by yourself, mime the actions of getting dressed in that costume, using an imaginary full length mirror. Do not be concerned wih playing a character, but simply have your body know what it is "wearing."

Then find a way to stand, walk, sit, and handle small props, if any. Be guided by the pictures, and remember that the attitudes they depict were normal and natural to those people in that time.

Next, choose three pictures and copy each of the attitudes of the body in turn. Then link the three by going directly or indirectly from one to another, without breaking the postural-gestural feeling. The challenge lies in passing from one attitude to another. Finally, if you can find a justification for the series of movements, use it and play out whatever circumstances you have invented.

CUSTOMS AND MANNERS

The middle ages were a time of great ceremony. Important houses had large numbers of retainers, mostly men, and ritual surrounded all daily activities. Everyone bowed or curtsied (they were called reverences or salutations) upon entering or leaving a room in which there were persons of superior or equal rank. One of inferior rank knelt on one knee to speak with a superior, or in offering a gift or giving food or drink. The great sign of respect of kneeling on both knees was reserved for the church; however, women might also do so to one of high rank, for it was immodest to separate the knees. Hats were worn indoors and out, and were removed for church, royalty, superiors, and upon introductions. Before a superior one replaced the hat only upon invitation.

Children were brought up formally; they addressed parents and others by title, and even waited upon parents and guests. Boys were often sent to royal or noble houses to act as pages and servants—these were not menial tasks— to receive an education. Also found in these houses were lords, knights, squires, and ladies-in-waiting, working there for the prestige of being attached to an important house.

Boys studied Latin, then perhaps law, theology, or medicine. In the 16th century the "new learning" included logic, rhetoric, Greek, Hebrew, and English. Girls were educated at home or in a neighboring convent, in various aspects of housekeeping. Marriage was primarily a union between two land holdings, for wealth was reckoned in land and buildings. Young men, unless allowed a part of the father's estate, had to become independent through a wife's dowry; this was a socially acceptable attitude. Girls married from age

13 on, and men generally in their late teens or early 20s. By 21 an unmarried young woman had no valid place in society except in a nunnery.

The code of courtly love was a light-hearted game, outlet for poetry and dalliance. The well-bred woman was decorous, moderate, restrained, and kept her hands occupied with handiwork when they were not folded or holding the skirt drapery. She never went out of doors alone, did not glance about or flutter or gaze other than at the ground before her. She spent her time embroidering, weaving, making herbal recipes and beauty potions, covering recipe books with silk or velvet, tending herbs and plants. The fireplace was her special corner; there she sewed, and perhaps read. Despite the above recipe for dependent domesticity, here and there a voice was raised to say that woman was equal to man, had as much moral strength and intellectual ability.

Daily life for men consisted in playing chess or cards, in hunting, hawking, sword-play, dicing, or betting. Women too hunted and hawked, and everyone danced. Music was an everyday affair, for a proper education for both included learning to play an instrument. Hawking was an upper class leisure sport, and wrestling was popular in the lower classes.

The kiss of greeting on the mouth was used among all persons as a demonstration of affection, of good will, or of bestowing honor, between men, women, and between the sexes. Clasping hands was not used in greeting, but as a pledge of honor or friendship. A mark of polite behavior was the custom of leading another by the hand, of either sex, as a special courtesy. For royalty, or a lady of great quality, the hand was carried on the back of the leading hand. Gloves were a symbol of authority: to give one was a sign of trust, to throw or hit with one was an act of provocation. Gloves had to be removed in church, to render homage, to dance, or to take someone's hand.

Meals were ceremonious; at table one used a knife, spoon, napkin, drinking vessel, and trencher (flat board on which to place food). Strangers and guests were accorded special privileges, and dinner could last for hours. Food was handed around in bowls; bowls and ewers of water were served before and after meals for handwashing. People chewed herbs and spices to sweeten the breath.

Well-bred persons refrained from indulging in any free, natural laughter for it was held to be unbecoming and even dangerous, for germs were thought to be airborne. These were superstitious times, and there were recipes for gaining love, for fidelity or infidelity, for easy child-birth. Certain jewels were thought to offer luck, protection, or chastity.

Moral distinctions were very clear: elegance, good breeding, gentleness, consideration for others, and courtly (not sexual) love were virtues. Faults were extravagance and show, rudeness, lack of consideration, and guilty love.

SALUTATIONS

MAN'S BOW: The right foot is carried to the back, weight remaining forward, and both knees bend. This is a modification of what one would do if one were to kneel. The body inclines slightly forward, head in line with the body, and the hat is removed with the right hand and held at the side, with the inside of the hat hidden. To recover, straighten the body and the front knee, bring the back foot to place and cover the head if that is permissible.

WOMAN'S CURTSY: Keeping feet and knees together, gently bend knees. Hands can pick up the front of the gown, or they can sweep back with palms forward, an offering gesture.

To kiss the hand of the sovereign: the subject kneels, takes the sovereign's hand on the back of subject's own, places the forehead on the back of the royal hand, then stands, bows or curtsies, and backs away.

The quick "bob" is done by servants and tradespeople to superiors, and does not elicit a like response. Passing bows are slighter versions of standing bows, used for greeting or acknowledging greetings while walking along a street or making one's way through a throng of guests. To kneel, step back with one foot and sink to the knee. Rise straight up by pushing with the toes of the back foot.

DANCES

The *farandole* is a line dance with a leader; the line can go anywhere, forming serpentines or making patterns. Joined hands are held low, and the basic step is simply a step-hop, with the free foot carried forward on the hop. It can be danced in a lively manner or with gentle dignity, depending on tempo and one's station in life. To form a serpentine, the leader doubles back along the line as often as desired. Other patterns: The first two people break off and form a bridge, the others pass under and the first ones join on at the end. Or: all raise their arms to form a series of arches; the leader starts under the next nearest arch (between second and third dancers) and threads in and out through all the arches as the line follows.

The *branle* (pronounced "brawl" from French *branler*, to sway) was popular well into the 18th century. Slow and stately, it is danced in a single line, clasped hands held low. All face center and move clockwise, "with the sun." The basic step consists of a double to the left and a simple to the right (also called a "single"). Double: Step side left, step next to it with right, step side left again, touch right foot close to left. You can say: step-together-step-touch. Simple, or single: Step side right, then touch left foot close to the right. The double takes four counts, the simple is done on counts five and six. On the two touches, counts four and six, the body turns slightly in that direction (left if going left, right if going right), and also sinks with a slight bend in the knees.

Some branle music is written in 4/4 rather than 3/4 time. For these dances do two doubles instead of a double and a simple; the second double, to the right, is smaller than the first one so that the line can progress in space to the left.

Other popular dances: tordion, morris dances, pavane, almain.

NON-CHARACTER IMPROVISATIONS

Performing the dances will help actors become familiar with the strange clothing and comfortable with the salutations. Improvising in period will do the same, and during the process actors should keep conversation to a minimum and make no attempt to initiate dramatic actions. Here are suggested circumstances of ordinary daily life.

AT A STREET MARKET In ones and twos, the women accompanied by relatives or servants, people make their way along the street lined with stalls. They greet others in passing, or more formally if they stop to talk; they look at the booths and their contents of laces, gloves, gifts, toys; at jugglers, acrobats, beggars, or clowns in the street. Couples walk together without touching, but if it is necessary to lead a lady he offers his hand, not arm. On occasion individuals lift a pomander (or take it from a servant) to the nostrils, to counteract noxious odors which "bring the plague."

IN THE GREAT DINING HALL, NEAR THE FIREPLACE The women are spinning, embroidering, or mixing herbal potions for medicine, cosmetics, or cooking. Men are relaxing after a hunt—talking, playing with dogs, drinking, checking weapons. Or everyone listens to a story-teller, or to one of the ladies reading from a book.

IN THE GARDEN OR FOREST They are gathering herbs which the women will use in making medicines, cosmetics, or for cooking. This could be an occasion for gentle flirtation.

AT AN INN Travelers arrive by horseback at an inn and stop for rest and refreshment. Several people can compose one party; others are traveling alone or accompanied. (Agree beforehand on the time of year.) They take drinks, perhaps warm themselves before the fire, make sure of the horses, weather, and possibility of highwaymen, then leave to continue their journey.

AT A BALL Guests enter the great hall, greeting and mingling. Some sit in small conversation groups. The next dance will be a pavane; men seek partners, exchange salutations, and lead the women to the dance area. After the dance they salute again and wait for the next, or leave the dance floor. Music for a farandole begins; all hurry to form a line to dance it.

CHARACTER IMPROVISATIONS

If a group is in rehearsal, some of the above improvisations can be played in character when the setting is appropriate to the play. Greetings would then reflect characters' relationships or feelings—servile, pleased, cool, anxious, arrogant, sentimental, or other appropriate coloration.

Young people at their first ball might watch carefully those slightly older, as guide to proper behavior. Two partners dancing, one might be in love with someone else.

Older characters might teach young ones about herbs or hunting as they work. The gathering of herbs might be used by lovers to snatch time together.

Specific plays or scenes in work will suggest other possibilities.

Early Miracle Play, rehearsed mime scene for four. This should be played simply, larger than life, with great dignity and conviction. Cast: a Heathen, a Statue of St. Nicholas, two robbers.

The image of St. Nicholas is in its shrine in the church. A rich heathen approaches, deposits his treasure at the feet of the statue so that the Saint can guard it for him while he goes off on a journey. As soon as the heathen has gone robbers enter, creep up to the shrine, and silently carry off the treasure. Soon the heathen returns; on finding his property has been stolen he flies into a rage; he threatens and wishes to beat the image of the Saint which had failed to protect his treasure. But upon this the image moves, descends from its niche, goes out and stands before the robbers. Terrified by the miracle the thieves return trembling to the church, bringing back all they had taken. The Saint's image returns to its niche. The heathen is transported with joy; he dances and blesses the image, and proclaims his conversion to the true faith by kneeling and crossing himself.

'Fore that brave Sun the Father of the Day,
Doth love this Earth, the Mother of Night:
And like a reveller in rich array,
Doth dance his galliard in his leman's sight,
Both back and forth, and sideways, passing light;
His princely grace doth so the gods amaze,
That all stand still and at his beauty gaze. . . .

Sir John Davies, "Dancings of the Air"

ELIZABETHAN/ JACOBEAN
1550-1640

THE TIMES

The Renaissance . . . re-birth that touched every aspect of life, letters, art, science, religion, and politics. Led by Italy, the artistic and intellectual center of Europe, the deep surging movement brought forth giants of art, science, culture, literature, humanism and exploration—and irreconcilable conflicts between old and new.

Under her brilliant queen England appeared to be conqueror of the known world, as she assumed the foremost position in a Europe that was exhausting itself in the Thirty Years' War. Internally she was locked in religious struggles that also reflected the conflict of changing relations between king and populace, between privileged classes and the emerging industrial middle class. Feudal class lines were penetrated when some of the newly rich middle class found possibilities for upward mobility into the titled and Court circles.

The monopoly on education by the church was diminishing since the invention of the printing press, but it was still a highly superstitious age that believed in magic.

The changes that occurred in the Renaissance extended to women, who could now enjoy certain civic and personal rights, including participation in the more widespread education. Many men and women believed in a greater equality, or at least less inequality, of the sexes.

England's Charles I could not stem the tide of the new concepts carried on the waves of the Renaissance and was washed away. In France, religious wars were the hardest fought, for the longest time, in all Europe, and culminated in the Edict of Nantes allowing freedom of religion. The country was ruled by Catherine de Medici, regent for three sons, until the shaky throne was taken by the Bourbons.

* * *

Thanks in part to the custom of producing plays as rhetorical exercises in the universities, and thanks also to Elizabeth I encouraging plays and masques, there existed in England a lively theatre tradition. Plays were given almost every day in the open air to numerous audiences of both tradesmen and the upper classes, and reflected the increasing freedom for individuality in dress and behavior. In Italy, England, and France the theatre was now nourished also by professional touring companies, and companies were attached to noble houses. Any actors not connected with a company were classed as rogues and vagabonds. The Renaissance companies that had fanned out from Italian courts and fairs since 1450, touring intensively especially in Western Europe, brought a renascence in theatre to the countries that it touched; it influenced everyone, including Shakespeare and Moliere, and opened Spain's Golden Age. The written plays, *commedia erudita,* had to compete with the *commedia dell'arte*, a semi-improvised, skilled professional theatre that played both serious and farcical pieces.

English playwrights made extensive use of dumb show (pantomime) before and between acts, as in *Jocasta* by Gascoigne and Kinwelmersh, and for special purposes such as Shakespeare's brilliant use of dumb show in *Hamlet*. Actors had to compete for audience attention with the elements, with spectators eating, drinking and wandering about, and with patrons often seated on the stage. Thomas Dekker mocked the gallant who chose to sit on the stage, "by which deed he could display good clothes, a proportionable leg, white hand, the Persian lock and a tolerable beard; act as guide to the play; get him a mistress or wife, be the judge and examiner of the play, actors, and poet; purchase the dear acquaintance of the boys; examine the players' lace and wager upon its authenticity."

Women appeared on stage in Italy and Spain, but not yet in England. Upper class Italian women and men played the roles of young lovers in professional touring companies. One of them, Isabella Andreini, attained a great fame because of her talent, virtue, and intellectual abilities. Italian courtesans attended the theatre in masks, as did the English female spectators, and sat by themselves in the best places.

Elizabethan plays were considered too vigorous for the French well-bred audience, which disapproved of all that blood and violence. Their tastes ran rather to translations from classical antiquity and to elegant translations/ adaptations assiduously turned out by French playwrights of the popular *commedia dell'arte*.

James I too encouraged amateur theatricals; the Jacobean plays reflected a former time, were filled with horror, bloodshed, and revenge. The earlier Stuart Masques, huge productions for the Court amateurs, were great pageants of speeches, songs, dances, stage effects, elaborate costumes, and masks, generally on themes from myth and legend. Then the Commonwealth and the triumph of Puritanism led to the 18-year blackout which abruptly cut down England's public theatre; when it rose again with Charles II it had changed profoundly, into Restoration drama.

Opera began in Italy as a multi-media event with music, chorale, lavish scenery and pastorale—but the music and scenery were all that interested the audience.

On the stage: *Commedia dell'arte*, playwrights Lope de Rueda, Cervantes, Lyly, Kyd, Lope de Vega, Marlowe, Shakespeare, Tirso de Molina, Dekker, Beaumont and Fletcher, Jonson, Webster, Calderon, and Corneille; actors Alleyn, Burbage and Kemp; designer Inigo Jones.

In the arts: Artists Cellini, Breughel, El Greco, Caravaggio, Rubens, Hals, Van Dyck, Velasquez, and Rembrandt; musicians Palestrina, Buxtehude, Byrd, Morley, Dowland, Monteverdi, and Frescobaldi; writers/poets Ronsard, Descartes, Butler, Milton, and Pascal.

THE CLOTHING

Hampering as the clothing was, it still permitted the swaggering lords of the earth and their ladies to dance the vigorous galliard, reputedly Elizabeth's favorite. The square Tudor silhouette was softened into that of a rounded square; clothes became refined and elegant, with silks and velvets, embroidery, precious buttons, furs, and lace. Makeup was used by both sexes. Wealth was purposely and proudly displayed in apparel, jewelry, horses, servants, and largesse, and the relaxation of the previous stiffness also showed in manners and movement.

Men wore various styles of breeches, and the doublet was padded. The ruff, which had begun modestly as a simple frill, became larger, starched, shaped, and ornamented; the wearers resisted all attempts to curb their excesses. Capes were draped dashingly over the left shoulder, and heels appeared on shoes and boots after 1558. Men wore their own hair; many were clean shaven while others wore small beards and moustaches. Accessories could be swords, canes, daggers, mirrors, gauntlets, purses, muffs, pomanders (apple-shaped caskets containing aromatic substances, to "ward off plague" or unpleasant odors), tobacco pouches, and the new, elegant watches.

Women's skirts retained the farthingale until early in the 1600s; thereafter skirts were still bulky and had to be managed without hauling them about by hand, but rather with small movements at the waist. The necessary little gliding steps were somewhat easier with the medium heels being worn. Bodices were stiffly boned, and decolletage and uncovered lower arms reflected the new relaxation. Accessories could be fans attached to the waist by a cord, pomanders, handkerchiefs, muffs, lockets, veils, sweet box, and masks, the last worn in public to protect the lady's reputation and her complexion. Women curled and dyed their hair. After 1630, patches on cheek or

neck were popular. Widows wore black, and covered their hair with a black veil.

A dandy might wear a really outsize ruff, would curl his hair, comb his beard, wax his moustache, and use perfume, the grooming often done in public.

Puritans wore the same garments as other people, but of plain, dark materials and devoid of trimmings. Women servants wore simple dresses, apron, cap, and kerchief. The men dressed in breeches and plain doublet of cloth or leather. Tradesmen and professionals had distinctive clothing, their occupations marked by color and by simple accessories of their crafts.

In the seventeenth century the relaxing of the silhouette continued, from the rounded square to an oval shape in trousers and sleeves, and thence to a soft drape by the time of Charles I. The doublet lost some padding, then became a loose jacket with lace ruffles. The full Jacobean skirt lightened also to a soft, billowing fullness. The ruff became smaller, and eventually was replaced by the deep lace collar, no longer hampering head and neck movement.

EXERCISE ON DRESS AND MOVEMENT

First, examine the drawings of the clothing; also look at costume books in the library (see the bibliography and/or your own library). Choose a picture and, working by yourself, mime actions of getting dressed in that costume, using an imaginary full length mirror. Do not be concerned with revealing character, but simply have your body know what it is "wearing."

Then find a way to stand, walk, sit, and handle small props, if any. Be guided by the pictures, and remember that the attitudes they depict were normal and natural to those people in that time.

Next, choose three pictures and copy each of the attitudes of the body in turn. Then link the three by going directly from one to another, without breaking the postural-gestural feeling. The challenge lies in passing from one attitude to another. Finally, if you can find a justification for the series of movements, use it and play out whatever circumstances you have invented.

CUSTOMS / MANNERS

Grace and decorousness were the desirable traits in this polite society, and at the same time it was a lusty, gutsy age. The Renaissance hero was a courtier, a poet, and a soldier. Adventuring and exploring were encouraged by the Queen. The French ideal was that of moderate and graceful gestural conduct, avoiding both "the immobility of statues and the restlessness of monkeys." The relaxation of the stiff clothes was echoed in manners with an acceptance of a certain "becoming negligence." Protocol was very precise, but observed somewhat naturally, with an air of ease.

Servants in noble houses were sometimes themselves young aristocrats, serving in an important house to receive an education.

The Age of the Courtier entailed tedious hours of hanging about the noble houses, gaming, gossiping, enjoying delightful entertainment, music, dancing; puzzling questions were propounded and ingenious games devised, all overlaid with witty repartee. Both men and women spent long hours on horseback, and men devoted much time to practicing sword play. Young people learned to walk, sit, bow, curtsy, and dance at the London dancing schools. Jonson's *Cynthia's Revels* poked fun at the affectations of some courtiers—those who overdid the ceremonies were subjects of ridicule. The English also loved to ape foreign fads, and this too was a target for the wits.

Courtship custom decreed that parents choose spouses for their children, who could legally marry at 12 for girls, 14 for boys. Actually they usually married at about 15–16 and early 20s, and the two were to be within an appropriate rank and status. All of Shakespeare's couples fall within these custom precepts. A betrothal was marked by a gift, often an heirloom, as was Othello's handkerchief given to Desdemona.

A kiss was common with and between the sexes, a custom which ended by the time of the Restoration. It often came at the end of a dance, was used as greeting, or as a ritual in betrothal or marriage ceremonies. Handclasps were not a form of greeting, but used as a pledge of friendship or agreement.

Hats were worn indoors and out, and conduct in the street included an elaborate etiquette concerning them: when to doff (do off)—before a superior, on greeting, or being introduced; when to don (do on), which depended on relationships and status, etc. Ladies wore masks, which were tied with ribbon or mounted on a holder, to the theatre and in public generally. Rings could be worn over tight-fitting gloves, or under them if the gloves were split to show the ring beneath. The glove had to be removed to take an offered hand. Amateur theatricals were popular, but a girl of good family would act or dance only before her family and friends.

Elizabeth I and other monarchs forbade dueling, but it was considered a sign of courage to flout the law. People crossed themselves before the altar, at news of death, at mention of witchcraft and plague, and upon sneezing (breath was life). To avert the evil eye they crossed two fingers on one hand, or crossed the two index fingers.

At social gatherings men left their cloaks and swords at the entry, but kept the dagger since it would be needed at table. Noon was the customary dining hour. To lead a lady by the hand, the man took her hand into his palm. But to royalty or high nobility he offered the back of his hand, on which the sovereign placed the royal fingers. Children were highly respectful: they removed their hats when speaking to an adult, or on being spoken to. They bowed and curtsied and kissed the parents' hands morning and night; kneeled and kissed hands to ask pardon, as Juliet would to her father, or for a blessing as Laertes to his father. No child or unmarried woman sat in the presence of parents unless given permission. Men and women sat gracefully, not so far back as to loll, with both feet on the floor, perhaps one arm on the chair and the other hand holding gloves, a flower, or handkerchief. Women's hands not otherwise occupied usually rested together, palms up, in the lap. If a rapier were worn, it had to rest alongside the body. At balls the sexes sat separately; either one could invite a partner to dance, which was never refused, and a return invitation was expected. Traveling was by horseback; the nobility had their own mounts, and others traveled by post horses from a network of wayside inns. All carried weapons, because of highwaymen.

The Fan. This was a weapon of another sort, with an infinity of use. It could be held; it could be dropped; it could hide, or reveal; draw attention or repel it; it could punctuate a phrase or draw it out lingeringly—altogether a teasing, tantalizing resource. There existed an entire pantomime language of the fan, with specific meanings attached to gestures: "we are watched," "follow me," "I love another," and many more. When sleeves were padded, the arm was curved out from the body and the fan deployed mainly from the wrist; looser sleeves permitted greater arm flexibility. Round fans were in vogue to about 1600, but folding ones came in around 1550. By the time of Charles I some fans were square, mounted on a stick, with lace eyeholes. The celebrated English actress Athene Seyler offers (1947) her practical ideas about fans, ideas suggested more by the theatrical logic of the fan than by historical research. To her the seventeenth century's shaking curls and bare bosoms called for flirting with a fan; the eighteenth century's more formal grace suggested a larger fan moving more slowly; and the Victorian fan would be smaller, demure, and suggest subtler shadings and shadowings of meaning.

SALUTATIONS

WOMAN'S CURTSY: Draw the left foot back into a slightly open third position. Bend both knees and incline the body slightly. Both heels remain on the floor unless a deep, ceremonious curtsy is called for, in which case the feet would be wider apart and the back heel would come up off the floor.

MAN'S BOW: Bring the left foot back to a comfortable fourth position with the weight remaining on the right leg, at the same time that the right knee bends; the weight then shifts to one's center, both knees bending. At the same time remove the hat with the right hand and incline

the body from the waist. The hat can be held at
the thigh, the inside hidden. On rising, the
weight moves forward to the front leg. One can
also place the hat under the left arm on the salutation, which would leave free the right hand to
make an offering gesture or to kiss the fingers
(see below), if desired. Take care to *place* the
moving foot to the back, not to slide it, for that
suggests a "scraping and cringing courtier."

The quick "bob" is done by servants and tradespeople to one of a higher
status, from whom a like response is not called for.

Bows and curtsies in passing are somewhat less ceremonious. To greet
someone on one's right, turn slightly toward them, and as the right foot takes
a step, bend the knee slightly. It amounts to a continuous walk with an
acknowledgement in the form of a knee dip.

To kiss the hand of a sovereign: the subject kneels, takes the sovereign's
hand, if it is offered, on the back of subject's own, places the forehead on the
back of the royal hand, then stands, bows or curtsies, and backs away.

The kissing of the fingers was fashionable in Court society from the late
sixteenth century to the Restoration. A gesture of courtesy, it accompanied a
salutation, or the giving or taking of objects such as a gift, a glove, or a
document. The right hand, curving inwards, was brought near one's own
lips, the back of the fingers was kissed without actually touching, and the
hand then gestured toward the recipient.

DANCES

The pavane had been popular since the previous period, and the Elizabethans
also favored the livelier dances like the galliard.

Of Spanish origin, the *pavane* is a slow, stately processional danced down
the center of a hall, often done by only one couple as an honor shown them.
The dance can contain many figures, but here is a simple version of only the
basic pavane step.

The lady is on the right of the man, and she rests her hand palm up in his
hand, his thumb lightly holding her hand in place, about waist high. She can
drop her outside hand to her side or lightly touch the farthingale if one is
worn; he can rest his left hand on his hip or his dagger hilt, if one is worn.

The basic step pattern consists of two simples (or singles) and a double. A
simple takes two counts: on count 1 step diagonally forward with the left foot;
on count 2 bring the right foot alongside, touching the ball of the foot to the
floor. For the second simple, repeat to the right, starting with the right foot.
The double takes four counts: on count 1 step diagonally forward with the left

foot (same as before); on count 2 join the right foot to the left putting weight on the right; on count 3 do the same as count 1, and on count 4 bring the right foot alongside, touching the ball of the foot to the floor (same as before). Thus the double amounts to taking three steps changing weight, and the fourth step without changing weight. Continue with two simples and a double. To review the whole: step-touch, step-touch, step, step, step-touch. Then reverse feet, starting with the right. Add to the above a gentle rise to the toes, then a slight bend of the knees each time the feet come together, which occurs once on each simple and twice on the double. Each step forward is done with the heel leading, body graceful and dignified without being stiff or affected.

The line of couples in double file, not too close upon each other's heels, can dance to the limit of the space, then wheel around in place to reverse direction. In order to wheel, the man steps backward on the double as the woman continues to go forward.

The galliard was a quick, energetic dance requiring rapid, neat footwork, the only dance performed bareheaded, hat in hand. Men danced it athletically yet with elegance, and women with a light and airy grace; it especially offered the gallant an opportunity to display flashy virtuosity. It was also called the five-step (cinq pas in French, sinkapace in Shakespeare) because of its pattern of four counts plus a syncopated fifth count on the sixth beat. The first line of "My Country Ti-is of Thee" ("God Save Our Gra-cious King") illustrates the rhythmic pattern.

Dancers face each other. On the first four counts make four jumps, alternating feet, kicking each foot forward. Then on two quick counts do a cadence on the syncopated beat by jumping onto the free foot, and on the sixth beat extend the weightless foot forward to an open fourth position, with a slight developé, the heel touching the floor. The steps of the cadence fall on the beats "of thee" in the song. The final attitude looks a bit like a bow, with body and arms in a presenting posture. Arm positions can vary. Both men and women can hold their arms diagonally down, and with a small presenting gesture of open palms on the cadence. Women can let their fingertips rest lightly on the farthingale, but not lifting skirts. Men can place hands on hips, opening them on each cadence. They can also hold both arms high, especially when performing a variation similar to a Highland fling.

After beginning the dance together, each one alternately dances a variation while the partner promenades admiringly in front of the dancer. Couples can dance moving forward and holding hands for the basic pattern (four kicks and a cadence) done four times, then face each other while each one alternates with a variation, then forward together again for four patterns, then facing for another variation, etc. Variations: (1) Body turns side to side on each kick, the arms swinging the opposite way in compensation. (2) Execute a full turn on the four kicks. (3) Kicks can be done front and back, using the same foot, changing feet, or any combination desired. (4) Women can do two quick *pas de basque* steps instead of the four kicks. Other variations can be invented by the actors.

Other dances of the time: bourré, basse dances, courante, saraband, gigue (jig), gavotte, rigaudon.

NON-CHARACTER IMPROVISATIONS

Performing the dances will help actors become familiar with the strange clothing and comfortable with the salutations. Improvising in period will do the same, and during the process actors should keep conversation to a minimum and make no attempt to initiate dramatic action. The following situations are those of ordinary daily life.

AT A STREET MARKET In ones and twos, women masked and accompanied by relatives or servants, people make their way along the street lined with stalls, greeting others in passing or more formally if they stop to talk; they look at the booths selling food, beverages, laces, toys, gloves, gifts; at jugglers or acrobats, beggars or clowns, fortune-tellers or quack doctors. When it is necessary to lead a lady, the man offers his hand, taking hers into his palm, glove off. On occasion, individuals lift a pomander (or take it from a servant) to the nostrils to counteract noxious odors which "bring the plague."

IN THE GARDEN For women. It being a fine day, the women have decided to remain out of doors to prepare herbs for cooking, for medicines, and for cosmetics. They have fresh and dried herbs, creams, and liquids, along with instruments and containers of glass and china. They also read to each other.

AT THE FENCING MASTER'S For men. During a rest pause in the fencing lesson the men stretch, limber up, chat, practice moves, check foils, etc.

AT AN INN Travelers have arrived at an inn by horse or by coach, and stop for refreshment and perhaps to change horses. People can travel in parties, singly (men), or with companions. After refreshing themselves, perhaps before the fire, then making sure of the horses, weather, and possibility of highwaymen, they leave to continue their journey.

AT THE GLOBE THEATRE In the hour before the play begins the audience gathers. The upper classes find their way to the boxes; perhaps they buy sweets or fruits from passing vendors. Gallants gather at the benches in the orchestra or on the stage, examining the women and each other's clothing, paying no attention to the common people behind them. It is a lively scene with much movement, until the play begins.

THE QUEEN'S PASSAGE Queen Elizabeth I arrives, preceded by gentlemen of the nobility, bare-headed and carrying the royal seals, sceptre, and sword of state. The Queen is flanked by a guard of honor, followed by titled ladies, two of them bearing her train.

Wherever she looks, the courtiers kneel on one knee; she stops to speak, or to receive a scroll; to some she offers her hand, a special mark of favor, which is kissed by the fortunate person. As the Queen nears the exit the Court cries "Long live Queen Elizabeth!" She turns graciously, replies "I thank you, my good people." And exits.

AT A BALL Guests enter the great hall, mingling and greeting each other. They find partners for a pavane, salute each other and the man leads the lady to the dance area. After the dance they salute again, and can add a kiss on the cheek. For the galliard to follow they can remain partners, or he can lead her back to her place and they find other partners. Refreshments can be taken between dances.

CHARACTER IMPROVISATIONS

Any of the above improvisations can be played in character when the setting is appropriate. Greetings might then reflect relationships or feelings—servile, cool, arrogant, sentimental, or whatever is suggested by the play.

Dancers at a ball can be in love with someone not their partner; Romeo and Juliet might dance a pavane, as could Kate and Petrucchio (it matters not at all that such a dance would not occur in the play—actors can find something of value out of the situation).

A lady with a fan seated between two gallants receives their attentions; one is welcome to her and the other is not, but she is too polite to be ungracious and only the fan reveals her feelings.

Pairs of lovers can gather herbs in the garden.

Disguise: Two young women decide to dress in their brothers' clothes so as to be able to go freely to where they might see the young men that interest them—perhaps to the theatre. With much laughter and teasing mockery they practice men's walks and poses. Each in turn takes the part of the absent swain as they enact how they'll meet, what they'll say, etc.

Two rivals find themselves at the fencing master's.

At an inn, one person recognizes a character who is traveling incognito.

Specific plays or scenes in work will suggest other possibilities.

Dumb Show from *Hamlet*, rehearsed mime scene. This should be played simply, larger than life, with great economy, dignity, and conviction. Cast: King, Queen, Claudius, two or three walk-ons. *Enter a King and Queen very lovingly; the Queen embracing him, and he her. She kneels and makes show of protestation unto him. He takes her up and declines his head upon her neck, lays him down upon a bank of flowers. She, seeing him asleep, leaves him. Anon comes in a fellow, takes off his crown, kisses it, and pours poison into the King's ears, and exits. The Queen returns, finds the King dead, and makes passionate action. The poisoner, with some two or three Mutes, comes in again, seeming to lament with her. The dead body is carried away. The poisoner woos the Queen with gifts; she seems loath and unwilling a while, but in the end accepts his love. Exeunt.*

. . .
Beauty and Joy, twin souls, should meet
To make that lovely miracle—
The perfect dance.

> Anonymous, "The Perfect Dance"

RESTORATION

1660 - 1700

THE TIMES

I t was now France's turn to come to the fore, thanks to her newly established centralized government. The iron fist and the velvet glove kept the 5000 willing and unwilling courtiers living at Versailles constantly and delightedly amused with a magnificent flowering of the arts. The Court of Louis XIV housed the finest collection of artists and artisans in music, theatre, painting, dance, carving, precious metals, jewelry, tapestries, architecture, and gardening that was possible. The French academies were established one by one between 1635 and 1671; among them the Académie Française to oversee the language; academies of science, of literature, and of dance, part of whose function it was to determine how the Court minuets would be danced, and which later gave the world the classic ballet.

England suffered successively The Plague, The Great Fire, and the deposing of James II, 1688. Charles II, raised in France and restored to the English throne, brought French taste, custom, manners, theatre and dress to England, and opened the way for the bouncy Restoration Comedy of Manners.

* * *

In France the Age of Reason was reflected in the theatre by the neo-classicism of Corneille and Racine. In the ideal *honnête homme*, imagination and passion were controlled and subjugated to reason. Racine's style was elegant and simple, with mathematical purity and beauty. Form and style were all-important, and even French tragedy was an elegant intellectual exercise.

53

In contrast, Moliere's early plays were *commedia dell'arte* farces; when he came to the Court, where he was a great favorite, his plays then assumed a greater three-dimensional complexity. His innovation was to people them with bourgeois characters rather than noble ones.

Elizabethan theatre had been proscribed by the Commonwealth; when the proscription was lifted in 1660 the suppressed frivolities plus Charles' importations from France resulted in the English Restoration stage, the Comedy of Manners consisting of wit, sexual intrigue, rakish behavior, and comment on Court doings. With it came the proscenium arch, orchestra pit, wings, curtain, lights, scenery, and women actors—the last enabling playwrights to increase the number of seduction, love, and gossip scenes. The broad Elizabethan audience too had changed, to an upper class patronage paying higher admission prices; the plays began to deal with subjects of interest to the rising bourgeoisie.

In both England and France, members of the audience were seated on the stage. In both countries only two legitimate, patented theatres were permitted; the others were obliged to offer a mixture of theatre forms.

Although opera had come in with the Renaissance, its form and style were Restoration. A baroque form imported from Italy in the seventeenth and early eighteenth centuries, it reflected the artistic interests of the nobility, in whose houses it had been born. Lavish scenic effects (the brothers Bibiena brought baroque architecture onto the stage), arias, and dance (the newly emerging ballet) were what the audience wanted.

On the stage: playwrights Corneille, Moliere, Dryden, Racine, Wycherly, Behn, Regnard, Vanbrugh, Congreve; actors the Bettertons, Bracegirdle, Cibber, Wilkes, Booth, Garrick, Siddons, Gwynne.

In the arts: writers La Fontaine, Pepys; musicians Lully, Corelli, Scarlatti, Purcell; painters Vermeer, Lancret; and architect Wren.

THE CLOTHING

Exuberant was the word for Restoration fashion. Curls, ribbons, puffs, flounces, feathers, lace, ruffles, buckles, garters, bows, furs, jewelry, gold and silver, were attached wherever they could cling. Elegance and artificiality were sought for. Cardinal Mazarin tried to curb the costly excesses which were leading to waste and debt, but the artisans and courtiers united against the laws. For all that the clothing is overdone, the actor must dominate it with delight, says Oxenford. The shape of the time was a baroque curve, like a great curled plume, a brilliant bold stroke made with dash.

Men wore great curled wigs, brimmed and plumed hats, or tricornes, often carried rather than worn. They sported cravats, wide cuffs, and layers of

cloth; shirt, doublet, coat, cape. The small amount of fullness at the arm-holes restricted arm movement. The coat needed a slit at the side or back in order to accommodate the sword, which now had a knuckle bow hilt. Beards and moustaches were disappearing, Louis XIV being clean-shaven. Accessories could be snuff boxes and handkerchiefs carried in the new-fashioned coat pockets, watches hung from the neck or in a waistcoat pocket, patches, pipes, muffs, pomanders (apple shaped caskets containing aromatic substances, to "ward off plague" or unpleasant odors), and canes.

The stiffly boned bodices of the women were tightly laced, and skirts were heavy and full. The swaying of the skirts had to be controlled with delicate maneuvering from the waist and by remaining centered in the skirt, particularly on coming to a halt. In order to sit, a woman allowed a portion of the skirt to move beyond the chair, then stepped back to sit on the chair edge. Her provocative low decolletage was meant to suggest that the bodice was about to slip off. Hair was worn in curls, or in huge wired arrangements in which one slept as best as one could. As accessories they could carry parasols, fans (see note in Ch. 3, p 46), masks for wear in public, patches, muffs, pomanders, canes, sweets boxes, and non-utilitarian aprons.

Both sexes wore heels, jewelry, makeup, patches, sported tall canes, and carried muffs hung from the neck or the waist. Fops also wielded fans.

EXERCISES ON DRESS AND MOVEMENT

First, examine the drawings of the clothing; also look at costume books in the library (see the bibliography and/or your own library). Choose a picture and, working by yourself, mime actions of getting dressed in that costume, using an imaginary full length mirror and an imaginary servant if you like. Do not be concerned with revealing character, but simply have your body know what it is "wearing."

Then find a way to stand, walk, sit, and handle small props, if any. Be guided by the pictures, and remember that the attitudes they depict were normal and natural to those people in that time. Gesture was flowing, sweeping, curving.

Next, choose three pictures and duplicate each of the attitudes of the body in turn. Then link the three by going indirectly from one to another, without breaking the postural-gestural feeling. The challenge lies in passing from one attitude to another. Finally, if you can find a justification for the series of movements, use it and play out whatever circumstances you have invented.

Because the upper arms were constricted, most movement was done by the lower arms. Practice a flourish of the wrist, which was used frequently, especially on giving or receiving an object. It can be done in either direction.

Men should practice sitting while wearing a sword, by giving a little tap to the hilt so that the blade flips the coat skirts open. Or, without a sword, slip open the coat skirts with the hands.

Snuff was used by both sexes, although it was somewhat daring for women to do so. It was expensive, so the lid was tapped to save any grains. After opening the lid, a pinch was taken with the right hand, the box lid closed with the left, and the snuff either carried directly to each nostril in turn, or placed in the hollow in the left hand between the thumb and forefinger and then carried to the nostrils. One did not sneeze, for that was bad form. Cuffs and shirt front were then flicked with a handkerchief, as the stains were hard to remove.

CUSTOMS / MANNERS

Customs and manners were as studied and elaborate as the clothing, and deliberately so, for the code of behavior was designed to mask feelings. Affectation was the desired attitude, performed with a studied nonchalance. Emotional or immoderate behavior was ridiculous and undesirable. They were frank about the affectation, everyone knowing it was simply form. Manners of the Court, which set the code, were often more extreme than the rest of society except, of course, for those "more royalist than the king" who devoted their energies to aping the Court. Women were not coy or arch, but openly immodest or provocative—again, as external form.

Louis' Court was heavily laden with protocol; who was allowed to sit in the Queen's presence, who had right to an armchair and who a stool, who was allowed to drive up to the Louvre—all prerogatives jealously fought for and guarded. At Paris, it was said, "women enjoyed much liberty and spent much money on dress; men were too great lovers of wine, female pleasures, and sports, seeing no court but the tennis court and no balls but tennis balls." At the Tuilleries Gardens one could find snacks, card games, ball games, skittles, and wrestling.

Recreation activities were balls, private dances, masques at Court, plays, card games, hunting, hawking, tennis, and courtesy visiting. At the theatre one paid for the entrance, the seats in a box, baskets of preserves, macaroons, and cooling drinks. When gentlemen took ladies for a walk in the pleasure gardens such as Vauxhall, they treated them to preserves and refreshing drinks. At dancing schools, which taught deportment as well as dances to young people, they stood them to snacks. London dancing schools were also frequented by married and unmarried ladies attending the evening dances. In the French Court, distinction in dancing was an aristocratic preserve, and a young bourgeois was warned to avoid excellence before the nobility. Many aristocrats appeared in the Court masques.

Not all the aristocracy spent their lives in recreation. Many managed their estates; some of the noble and upper class women established hospitals, devoted themselves to nursing, visiting the sick, and helping the poor. Others followed intellectual pursuits, like Christine of Sweden who lived in Rome surrounded by philosophers and writers. However, intellectuality in women was considered unsuitable.

Daily activities for women included sewing, knitting, embroidering, making lace, painting, making beauty potions and creams which, with coloring added, were put into little glass or china bottles, jars, or pots. They dried flower petals to make scent bags. For men, time was spent in hunting, practicing fencing, dancing, being fitted for clothes, shoes, and wigs; they cleaned pistols, tested swords, and mended whips. Personal grooming favored the use of perfumes over that of soap and water, and perfumed handkerchiefs kept offensive odors at bay.

Salutations were performed before superiors, on being introduced, and upon entering a room where peers or superiors were present. The etiquette of walking abroad and greeting persons was very elaborate, governed by such factors as who had the wall side, or the right side, from what distance to greet someone; the delicate jockeying for position between equals meeting in public depended also on how many retainers were looking on to report the one-up-manship.

Hosts greeted visitors from varying distances, according to their respective stations; it ranged from simply remaining in the room to going a distance along the road to meet the visitor. Lower classes went arm in arm, but to lead a lady a gentleman offered his hand, with a baroque flourish of the wrist and ending with the index finger uppermost, allowing the lady to rest her fingertips lightly upon it, after executing a graceful wrist flourish on her own part. Kissing as a form of greeting was going out of fashion by the end of the century. Still popular was the simulated kissing of the fingers on giving or receiving an object, with the glove removed, now performed with the flourish of the wrist.

If a lady of quality was attended by other ladies, one did not greet them until the superior had left—and then one must apologize for the delay. Nor did one take snuff before any person of honor, for he had the privilege of offering it himself. Hats were worn indoors and out, and while dancing. Guests removed their hats upon bowing and did not replace them unless pressed to do so by the host. A handclasp was used only as a pledge of friendship or agreement. Tobacco was smoked only at home.

By 1677 so many young men went into business or professions that women were being employed as servants.

Travel was done by coach, and in Europe travelers would hire a guide to deliver them safely at their destinations; guides were often rogues, but they knew the correct charges, the inns, and the language. When a coach arrived at an inn the servants rushed out to minister to the travelers, knowing that the tip depended on it. The innkeeper's wife, family (both boys and girls) and servants all could carry luggage, serve meals, clean, make beds, care for the horses, and waken the passengers in the morning.

SALUTATIONS

MAN'S BOW: Remove the hat with the right hand, place it in the left hand or under the left arm. Step forward on the right foot (or alternatively place the left foot back) into fourth position, knees turned out. With weight on the front foot, bend the front knee, then shift weight to the back leg and keep both knees bent; incline the body; both feet remain flat on the floor. The right arm can sweep forward, down and back, but not past the line of the body. On rising, the hand can be kissed to the one to whom the bow is directed. The weight can remain on the back leg  or move forward to the front one. If the hat remains in the right hand, it can be swept back on the bow, with the inside showing. The attitude of the legs was meant to show off a gentleman's fine calf, called "making a leg" in contemporary literature.

 WOMAN'S CURTSY : With the legs turned out, make a small preliminary step to either side, draw the other foot in to join the heels in first position; bend both knees and incline the body slightly. If it is to be a deeper curtsy, to show deference to a high personage, come to a fourth position and let the back heel come off the floor.

Men servants, on performing a duty and on leaving a room, bowed the head and body, with heels together. Women servants curtsied (a simple bob) on speaking to employers or any superior. Tradesmen bowed on being given an order, innkeepers on greeting visitors, etc.

To kiss the hand of a sovereign: the subject kneels, takes the sovereign's hand, if it is offered, on the back of subject's own, places the forehead on the back of the royal hand, then stands, bows or curtsies, and backs away.

Passing bows are slighter versions of standing bows, used for greeting or acknowledging greetings while walking along a street or making one's way through a throng of guests.

DANCES

The *courante* was popular for a long time; Elizabethans had danced it with jumps and hops (corranto); then the jumps became smooth gliding steps and it was danced well into the eighteenth century as the courante. Couples dance holding hands, the woman on the right, and move clockwise in a large circle.

The basic pattern consists of two simples (singles) and a double, just as in the pavane, but the tempo is livelier. Step forward on the left foot on count 1, quickly bring the right toe alongside with a tiny shift of weight, and change weight back onto the left foot on count 2: step-ball-change. Do the same with the right foot, and those are the two simples. Then take two gliding steps forward on counts 5 and 6: left, right; and repeat the first simple on counts 7 and 8—that is the double. Now the right foot is free, and the whole is repeated starting with the right. The above can be danced to a 4/4 or 6/4 rhythm.

An easy courante can be danced as follows: two basic patterns forward, then two circling away from each other, then two forward again, and two patterns circling around each other. Repeat as long as desired.

In this simple version of a *minuet*, the basic step is similar to the courante but slower and in six counts. It consists of two singles and two walking steps: Step forward with left foot on count 1, bring the right foot to touch heels in first position and with a small knee bend on count 2. Repeat with the right foot on counts 3 and 4. Take two walking steps forward: left, right, on counts 5 and 6. This basic step does not alternate. Partners are arranged in a double line down the center of the hall, women as always on the right. The arms are held in "garland position" (as though carrying a garland) which Rameau instructs as follows: "Stand with feet together, tips of fingers of both hands resting lightly on the diaphragm. Keep the elbows in place and open the lower arms to the sides." The hands face forward.

This minuet can be danced using the same design as for the courante above: two patterns moving forward, two circling away, two forward, and two circling around. In the last one partners can hold hands.

Other dances of the time: sarabande, gigue, gavotte, bourée, rigaudon, passepied.

NON-CHARACTER IMROVISATIONS

Performing the dances will help actors become familiar with the strange clothing and comfortable wih the salutations. Improvising in period will do the same, and during the process actors should keep conversation to a minimum and make no attempt to initiate dramatic action. The following situations are those of ordinary daily life.

AT A STREET MARKET In ones and twos, women masked and accompanied, people make their way along the street lined with stalls, greeting others in passing or more formally if they stop to talk. They look at the booths containing food, beverages, laces, toys, gloves, gifts, etc., at jugglers, acrobats, beggars, clowns, fortune-tellers, and charlatans. If it is necessary to lead a lady, the man takes off his glove and offers his hand with a flourish of the wrist; she lightly places her fingertips on his hand.

THE COACH Six persons install themselves in a public coach, in two rows facing each other. Most are strangers to each other, are loaded down with luggage which must be disposed of, and clothes are bulky. It is a long journey and people become tired, hungry, irritated, or bored. Finally they reach their destination.

AT THE THEATRE People arrive for an evening performance at a public theatre. There is an entrance fee, another for a box, and vendors hawk sweets and cookies. Those sitting in boxes are usually anxious to be seen, and there is much greeting and gossiping before the play begins, which is said to be a thinly-disguised farce involving a prominent personage.

AT HOME In small family groups of four or five, spend the afternoon in typical pursuits: women at handiwork, or in drying flowers or herbs, men with weapons or being fitted for wig or coat. Some may read, or write letters. Servants are given instructions, or sent on errands.

IN THE MINISTER'S ANTE-CHAMBER To the reception room of the Minister who grants patents and privileges, each person arrives to present his or her petition. A secretary (imaginary) sits near the big double doors of the Minister's office. Each one addresses the secretary quietly, exchanges salutations with any acquaintances, and waits to be called into the presence. A certain amount of coming and going of couriers and messengers creates an atmosphere of tension and anticipation, with most people wondering what the others are there for.

AT A BALL Guests arrive at a ball, where servants take the outer clothing. Enter and bow or curtsy to the assembled company. Wander through the throng, greeting others in passing or more formally. Guests are seated; the men find partners, bow to request the dance, the lady rises, curtsies, and is led to the dance area. They exchange salutations at the beginning of the dance, at the end, and return to her seat or to the refreshment table. Or he brings a cooling drink to her.

CHARACTER IMPROVISATIONS

Any of the above improvisations can be played in character when the setting is appropriate. Greetings would reflect the characters' feelings or relationships— servile, cool, arrogant, sentimental or whatever is suggested by the play.

Dancers at a ball can be in love with someone not their partner. On a split stage, two young lovers can practice how they will act when next they meet. During a concert in the salon, guests can listen, take refreshments, move about, use fan language, seek out or avoid, all in accordance with their obvious or covert relationships.

Minuet for *Way of the World*. Mirable and Millamant are in the center, surrounded by Lady Wishfort, Marwood, Mrs. Fainall, Fainall, Witwoud, Petulant, then Sir Wilfull and Sir Rowland. They dance with each other, in couples, changing partners continually after four dance patterns. They react to each new partner according to their relationships in the play.

Specific plays or scenes in work will suggest other possibilities.

Tomorrow will be my dancing day.
I would my true love did so chance
To see the legend of my play,
To call my true love to my dance.
Sing Oh! my love, Oh! my love, my love, my love, my love,
This I have done for my true love. . . .

Anonymous, "The General Dance"

EIGHTEENTH CENTURY

1700 - 1800

THE TIMES

The century spanned wide extremes as it encompassed the Age of Rococo and the Age of Reason; Mme. Pompadour and Voltaire; lavish living with an after-me-the-deluge attitude confronted dirt, stink and the gallows; wars proliferated; royal houses toppled. Russia and Prussia came out of isolation for their share of aggrandizing. The American colonies/United States were the battleground for rival colonial powers. All Europe was involved in warring of one kind or another, transforming the continent politically and socially. The ideas of the Arcadians, the Enlightenment, Voltaire and the Encyclopedists, calling for Reason and Justice, were justified when the American and French Revolutions shook and changed the world.

There was a general freeing of precise and rigid form, as seen in the adoption of the asymmetrical rococo style, a swing away from imposing grandeur in music, stage, and dress, in favor of light elegance, pointing the way to the still later Romantic movement. Art and intellectual life deserted the Courts in favor of salons and coffeehouses; art and art criticism were now offered to the public.

The plays were often bourgeois versions of the formal Restoration drama, but a loosening and warmth were becoming acceptable; the growing middle classes liked pathos and sentimentality, and melodramas were just their cup of tea. The star system—for it was a time of great virtuoso performers—encouraged pyrotechnics; lighting improved, stage effects became more elaborate and scenery more realistic. Actors had traditionally used their personal finery for stage costumes, however inappropriate, but now a few players favored costumes suitable to period and character. Mrs. Siddons was the first woman player to do so, Macklin was the first to use a Scots tartan in *Macbeth*, and the convention became custom.

Voltaire and Garrick cleared the stage of spectators, a step made easier by proscenium stages. Special contributions of eighteenth century dramatists were: the Town Gallant and the Town Miss (the gossiping fop and affected dame), heroes who were neither statesmen nor of the nobility, star vehicles, and elaborate stage mechanics. Most drastic were the opera reforms beginning with Gluck, leading to the integrated (as compared with disparate elements) *opera-comique,* folk-opera or song-play. The highly successful *Beggar's Opera* had its prologue delivered by an actor playing a beggar, a parody of grand opera's customary prologue given by a mythological figure, and was a general lampoon of Italian opera, Court, and government.

On the stage: playwrights Congreve, Farquhar, Gay, Marivaux, Goldsmith, Goldoni, Lessing, Beaumarchais, Sheridan; actors Cibber, Woffington, Garrick, Siddons, Riccoboni, John Kemble, and Talma; composer Gluck.

In the arts: musicians Vivaldi, Handel, Scarlatti, Bach, Pergolesi, Haydn, Gabrielli, Boccherini, and Mozart; painters Lancret, Watteau, Hogarth, Boucher, La Tour, Rousseau, Reynolds, Gainsborough, Fragonard, Goya, and Vigée-Lebrun; writers Addison, Steele, Voltaire, Johnson.

THE CLOTHING

Despite Dr. Johnson's remark that "fine clothes are good only as they supply the want of other means of procuring respect," the merry chase for fashion went on. The furbelows of the Restoration were replaced with simpler, cleaner lines and lighter weight fabrics; a certain restraint, compared with the lavishness of the previous age, favored silks and satins, slender canes and vertical wigs. The bold, broad Restoration flourish was refined to a light, graceful delicacy. Both sexes used makeup, wigs, and corsets.

Men, fully as style conscious as women, often wore wigs, but slowly they dispensed with them in favor of their own hair. With lighter fabrics clothing followed the lines of the body. Knee breeches were tight, and by the end of the century were held up with suspenders. Sleeves were more comfortable. Coats were knee length and varied in width; their skirts were stiffened and therefore had to be lifted aside in order to sit; the skirts also narrowed eventually to become coat tails. Pockets appeared in coats, which helped in carrying accessories. Either greatcoats or capes were worn, and the tricorne hat, point worn over the left eye. Heels were low. In the latter part of the century appeared the stock, a muslin band fastened in back, sometimes trimmed with a narrow black ribbon. Men's accessories were rings, watches, canes, snuff boxes (see Ch. 4, p 58), pipes, muffs, handkerchiefs, patches.

Women began the century by affecting a more natural coiffure, with ornaments in the hair, or the wearing of caps at home; later on elaborate wigs became fashionable and for some the hair became the single most important feature of eighteenth century fashion. Sleeves shortened to elbow length, with lacy falling ruffles. Hoops were out, then in, and became optional in the second half of the century. For formal occasions the side paniers, like the Spanish farthingale, were often used. With the hoop skirts women again had to walk with small, smooth, gliding steps in order to keep the hoop under control. Low necks and tight, boned bodices were popular, and the inflexible bodices sometimes resulted in "the vapors" or faintness.

Fans (see Ch. 3 p 46) reached the height of popularity and their manufacture was an important industry in England. In the hands of a woman they gave endless opportunity for an infinite variety of expression, and the eighteenth century was sensitive and knowledgeable regarding this important fancy. Other accessories were watches, cosmetics boxes containing cosmetics, beauty spots, candies, perfumes; also muffs, handkerchiefs, patches, long gloves, mitts, pomanders (apple shaped casket containing aromatic substances, to "ward off the plague" or unpleasant odors), parasols, masks for carnivals and balls. On their heads they wore mobcaps, hoods, straw Leghorn shepherdess hats tied under the chin; and a black velvet ribbon was tied around the throat.

First, examine the drawings of the clothing; also look at costume books in the library (see the bibliography and/or your own library). Choose a picture and, working by yourself, mime actions of getting dressed in that costume, using an imaginary full length mirror and an imaginary servant if you like. Do not be concerned with revealing character, but simply have your body know what it is "wearing."

Then find a way to stand, walk, sit, and handle small props, if any. Be guided by the pictures, and remember that the attitudes they depict were normal and natural to those people in that time. Next, choose three pictures and copy each of the attitudes of the body in turn. Then link the three by going indirectly from one to another, without breaking the postural-gestural feeling. The challenge lies in passing from one attitude to another. Finally, if you can find a justification for the series of movements, use it and play out whatever circumstances you have invented.

Practice the flourish of the wrist and of the lower arm, the "pleasing effect of which manner of moving is seen when a snuff box or fan is presented gracefully and gently," says Hogarth.

One way to control movements of a hoop skirt is to walk tracing an S-curve from one point to another. This helps to keep the body's center of balance centered in the hoop. It is very like going through a doorway in a skirt wider than the door; have one side of the hoop skirt pass the door frame, then turn the body gently to let the other side clear the door frame. The same S-curve can be used by both sexes in walking from chair to fireplace, table to door, etc.

Precision exercise for movement and speech: Oxenford states that for the eighteenth century "diction has to be precise but not affected (except in the case of fops), and the integration of speech and movement exceedingly accurately timed." The following exercise is a drill for coordinated timing, not necessarily to be used for all characters or every situation on stage. Take any line and say it with a corresponding move of any kind, so that the line and the gesture or movement begin at the same time and end at the same time. Do this several times, changing lines and changing movement.

CUSTOMS / MANNERS

The emphasis on form and on the primacy of reason continued from the previous century, but somewhat softened. A sense of lightness permeated everything: lighter weight clothing, sophisticated behavior, short and witty sentences, higher heels, and slender canes. Details of clothing were simplified and a certain relaxation in manners was initiated by an upper class which could deliberately disregard rigid rules. Actually, eccentricity was encouraged and admired.

69

Education of young ladies consisted mostly of deportment, social graces, domestic skills, and handiwork. It was "pedantic" for a woman to pronounce a difficult word correctly, hence a Mrs. Malaprop; women in intellectual pursuits tended to be ridiculed slightly.

English smart society lived in London, Bath, or other resorts or watering places. They spent their time in coffee houses or the theatre, and their gossiping, foppery, and affectation were favorite themes in Sheridan's plays. Tea and the tea table appeared; the hostess poured, added sugar and cream on request, and handed the cups around. An easy manner and agreeable negligence were desirable, since "good breeding shows most where it appears least." Both sexes used snuff, but only men smoked.

Deportment, which meant standing, walking, posture, and salutations, was taught in the dancing schools along with the dances. Men were beginning to remove their hats indoors. The tricorne was removed by grasping the brim with the right hand and letting the hat fall to the side, with the inside showing to display its cleanliness. On replacing it, one was careful not to let the hand or arm cover the face. The tricorne was worn low in front, with the point above the left eye. Musk and civet compensated for the rarity of bathrooms, and cologne water was popular throughout the world as a perfume and also as a remedy for headache, the vapors, and indigestion. The kissing of the fingers was now curtailed to a simple circular gesture toward the one being saluted. The dining hour was advanced, to 2 or 3 o'clock in the country, 4 or 5 o'clock in the city. Dinners were long affairs, and daytime snacks frequent.

Children could romp among themselves, but were expected to observe adult rules of behavior with family and friends. They were attended by nurses, tutors, and governesses; they saluted parents and other adults, waited for permission to sit; they were to stand if speaking or being spoken to, and were taught to be courteous to servants. For all the rigid class distinctions, there was a good deal of familiarity between mistress and maid, master and man.

Visiting was less formal; one could sit with work in hand and engage in cheerful conversation. One bowed or curtsied on entering a room, on greeting or meeting someone, on taking leave, and before and after a dance. Smiling was proper but "immoderate" laughter was "low and silly." Handclasps were not used as greeting, but as a pledge of friendship or agreement. Women were counseled to avoid all motions of the head, all wanton or sidewise glances, any ogling, winking or dimpling, and to avoid conceit and affectation. They spent their time at needlework, especially needlepoint for chairs, cushions, samplers, and firescreens, using a small round frame or large standing one; also in visiting, gossiping, cards, reading, singing, and playing the spinet or harpsichord. For men there were billiards, cards, checkers, horseracing, hunting, cock fighting, coffee houses, and visiting. Gambling was widespread, with all classes and in all places. In theory Sunday was strictly observed.

Men stood up when ladies entered the room or approached, or when a lady stood up, and remained standing until the lady left or sat down again. They opened and closed doors for them. Young women stood when an older woman entered. Chaperones sat with their young ladies at dances; the man seeking a dance partner bowed to the chaperone, then to the lady; she curtsied, they danced, and when they returned the man bowed to each one. And brought them drinks.

SALUTATIONS

WOMAN'S CURTSY: It remained the same as in the previous period. Take a small preliminary step to either side, bring the other foot in to join the heels in first position, bend both knees and incline slightly. The hands can remain crossed in front, or let fall to the sides, or a fan can be held in the right hand. Eyes are lowered, and raised when the knees straighten.

MAN'S BOW: Simplified manners simplified this salutation. The bow could be done either forward or to the side. To bow for-

ward, place either foot to the front and at the same time bend the back knee slightly and incline from the waist. Remove the hat at the beginning of the bow. To recover, straighten body and knee, and shift weight forward to the leg that first moved. Alternative: step to either side, bring the free foot to a fourth position back, taking the weight as the knee bends. Recover as above.

For a passing bow the hat was simply lifted; women nodded in acknowledgement.

DANCES

The *minuet* (see Ch. 4, p 61) retained its popularity. Other dances were the gavotte, gigue (jig), and canaries.

NON-CHARACTER IMPROVISATIONS

Performing the dances will help actors become familiar with the strange clothing and comfortable with the salutations. Improvising in period will do the same, and during the process actors should keep conversation to a minimum and make no attempt to initiate dramatic action. The following situations are those of ordinary daily life.

AT A STREET FAIR In ones and twos, women accompanied, people make their way through a village fair, past stalls containing toys, laces, jewelry, gingerbread, sewing implements, lotteries, and music; there are mountebanks, tumblers, clowns, rope dancers, magicians, and exhibits of drolls, wild beasts, puppets, monsters, giants, and dwarfs. One could throw for prizes or stop in the coffee houses, taverns, or eating houses. If it is necessary to lead a lady, the gentleman takes off his glove and offers his hand, on which she lightly places her fingertips. They wander around, enjoying the sights and greeting others in passing or more formally if they stop to talk.

THE COACH Six persons install themselves in a public coach, in two rows facing each other. Most are strangers to each other, are loaded down with luggage which must be disposed of, and clothes are bulky. It is a long journey and people get tired, hungry, irritated, or bored. Finally they reach their destination.

AT AN ART GALLERY OPENING People arrive for the opening of an exhibit by a fashionable painter. They wander through the gallery, as much to see each other as to see the pictures, and to be seen. The painter is present, receiving his friends and admirers.

THE TEA TABLE The family enters to take tea; on the table are: silver teapot (use actual water), silver milk jug, teaspoons, cups and saucers, sugar bowl and tongs. The hostess pours, asking each if they want milk or not, one lump or two, and the teacups are handed around. There are also small cakes and cookies on china plates or silver salvers. A servant might bring in a calling card, then usher in a visitor. One might ring for a servant to put coal on the fire, or sweep the hearth, or draw the curtains. Teacups are handed around by the butler on a formal occasion, a maidservant if less so, and by the gentlemen if the occasion is quite informal.

AT A BALL Guests arrive at a ball, let servants take the outer clothing, enter and bow or curtsy to the assembled company. They wander through the throng, greeting others in passing or more formally. Guests are seated; the men find partners, bow to request the dance; the lady rises, curtsies, and is led to the dance area. They salute each other at the beginning of the dance, at the end, and return to her seat or to the refreshment table. Or he brings a cooling drink to her.

CHARACTER IMPROVISATIONS

Any of the above improvisations can be played in character when the setting is appropriate. Greetings might then reflect characters' relationships or feelings—servile, cool, arrogant, sentimental, or whatever is suggested by the play.

Dancers at a ball can be in love with someone not their partner. A lady uses a fan to encourage or repel suiters. An unexpected meeting takes place at a street fair or in a coach. Tea time comes immediately after a tense family argument.

Specific plays or scenes in work will suggest other possibilities.

I love the jocund dance,
The softly-breathing song,
Where innocent eyes do glance,
And where lisps the maiden's tongue. . . .

William Blake, "Song"

Romantic

1780 - 1840

THE TIMES

In this short period the old and new, classicism and romanticism, overlapped as one replaced the other. The French Revolution changed everything—"map, manners, and modes." The country was experiencing the great political shifts and agonies of The Terror, the Directoire, the Napoleonic Empires, and the Restoration. England assumed ascendancy, literature flowered, trade and manufacturing expanded, and the Industrial Revolution turned the wheels of industry and created havoc among the displaced working hands.

Romanticism, by which name this period is known, was expressed in a passionate return to nature, character, soul, and truth, and a rejection of rigid form and intellectualization. Gothic, Oriental, antique and sentimental subjects mingled with the spirit of individuality and freedom in all the arts; poets wrote paeans to beauty and to human rights; the struggles for independence were supported by Lafayette (who had also helped the American Revolution), Chateaubriand, and Lord Byron. Artistic and intellectual life flourished and the dream of Liberty, Equality, Fraternity was carried to all parts of the world. Nature was the god and Rousseau was his prophet.

Falconet placed his wildly prancing carved horses on rough stone; French formal gardens turned into English informal ones; waltz replaced minuet and piano the harpsichord; the "simple, noble life" popularized folk opera, children's songs and literature, *Sturm und Drang*, and a wave of amateur practitioners in the arts. The newly rich collected paintings and embarked on conspicuous consumption to rival the Court of Louis XIV. Gas for illumination arrived, along with the telegraph and steam power. Over this ferment and foment, the three-four lilt of the waltz was said to be carrying the younger generation to perdition.

* * *

The stage too reflected the co-existence of the Age of Reason and display of feeling; the two were epitomized by Kemble, classicist, and Kean, romanticist. The playwrights wrote sentimental, passionate pieces involving middle class characters. A player's fashionable personal wardrobe no longer served for the stage, and appropriate costuming became the rule. Gas lighting permitted actors to move freely in space. Grand opera was charged with vitality as it continued the reforms begun by Gluck. Romantic historical subjects, folk heroes, violent plots and democratic aspirations molded the baroque opera to the era of industry and commerce. England saw the start of a hardy tradition, the Grand Comic Christmas Pantomime.

On the stage: playwrights Sheridan, Dumas, and du Musset; actors Siddons, Talma, Kemble, Kean, Rachel, Macready, Deburau, Grimaldi, Booth, Vestris; composers Meyerbeer, Verdi, Berlioz, Donizetti.

In the arts: painters Goya, David, Blake, Ingres; musicians Beethoven, Boccherini, Rossini, Schubert, Strauss, and Schumann; writers Goethe, Schopenhauer, Schiller, Burns, Wordsworth, Coleridge, Austen, Byron, Shelley, Keats, Stendahl, Balzac, Hugo, Sand, Gogol, Dickens, the Brontes, Hazlitt, and Hunt.

THE CLOTHING

The Napoleonic wars had two effects upon the world of fashion: clothing began to be less differentiated between classes, and the center of men's fashion moved from Paris to London, where it has remained. However, during the Directoire Napoleon encouraged the French, as an economic measure, to change from hand weaving to the new machines, and France eventually resumed her position as world center for women's fashion. The desired hourglass silhouette applied to both men and women. Fashion decreed appropriate dress for times of day or night: morning coat, morning dress, riding dress, ball gown, evening jacket, tea gown, etc.

Men's clothing continued to become simpler, if not more comfortable. Men wore their own often unconfined hair, and a top hat or cocked hat. Clothes conformed to the body; coat sleeves were moderate forms of women's leg-o'-mutton sleeves and offered more play for the arms; corsets were not unknown. Stocks and high collars remained and intricately-tied ties required lessons to learn their mysteries. Breeches were still worn but slim, tight, full length pantaloons were replacing them; by 1810 pantaloons were somewhat looser. Tailcoats, of varied length, were in favor; flat-heeled pumps and boots were the footwear. Waistcoats were either restrained or fanciful, made of velvet, satin, or embroidered silk. The overcoat with cape attached later became the coachman's uniform. The first suggestion of returning whiskers was evident, and men now wore no scent. Accessories: signet rings, watches

and fobs, cigars, sword-sticks, handkerchiefs, quizzing glass (see below), gloves, stocking purses, boutonnieres, cane or umbrella.

Women's clothing swung from one extreme silhouette to another. French fashions followed a Roman revival in the form of a simple, daringly revealing Empire gown, a long stole worn over the forearms; with it went a simple coiffure modelled on Greek and Roman styles, at times covered with a poke bonnet. Flat slippers or "Roman" sandals completed the costume. Thus women were temporarily freed of stays, until the next fashion change, popular throughout Europe, put them back in corsets for the hourglass silhouette composed of huge leg-o'-mutton sleeves, tiny waist, and hoop skirts or starched petticoats. Heels were low or non-existent and skirts were ankle length. One saw a dizzying variety of hats, from military shakos to shepherdess Leghorns. Ladies looked dashing in velvet riding habits, tricornes or shakos, and gauntlets. Trains worn on formal occasions were held up for dancing by a loop of ribbon on the little finger. Amelia Bloomer hoped that women would accept her style of uncorsetted bodies, jackets, and skirts worn over long full breeches; she failed, until the bicycle craze later required bloomers for women riders. Women's accessories: parasols, fans (see Ch. 3, p 46), gloves, mitts, locket-watches, bonnets, veils, reticules, large muffs, shawls, mantles, scarves, smelling bottle, jewelry, and band boxes to carry caps to parties.

We retain today some vestigial remnants from the period: the coachman's coat, the French Academy dress uniform, the bellhop uniform, the Quaker bonnet, Uncle Sam suit, West Point shako, riding breeches, three plumes for Court presentation, Eton jacket, formal tailcoat, and livery.

EXERCISES ON DRESS AND MOVEMENT

First, examine the drawings of the clothing; also look at costume books in the library (see the bibliography and/or your own library). Choose a picture and, working by yourself, mime actions of getting dressed in that costume, using an imaginary full length mirror. Do not be concerned with revealing character, but simply have your body know what it is "wearing."

Then find a way to stand, walk, sit, and handle small props, if any. Be guided by the pictures, and remember that the attitudes they depict were normal and natural to those people in that time.

Next, choose three pictures and copy each of the attitudes of the body in turn. Then link the three by going indirectly from one to another, without breaking the postural-gestural feeling. The challenge lies in passing from one attitude to another. Finally, if you can find a justification for the series of movements, use it and play out whatever circumstances you have invented.

CUSTOMS / MANNERS

The reign of form and the *honnête homme*, of self-control, grace, measure, and reason, was ending and *l'âme sensible*, the sensitive soul or spirit, was free to display passion and overt emotionalism. The code of behavior was less mannered, but still highly determined by precepts of good and bad taste. Respectability was the governing principle. Ostentation was vulgar and to be shunned, while courteous behavior was easy and unaffected. One was taught to be dignified but not proud, affable and not mean, elegant but not affected. Books on etiquette were now aimed at the middle class, and dancing schools taught posture and courteous exchange as well as dances.

In France the manifestations of sensitivity were often truly motivated, but among a few it was an artificial magnification of feeling. Vehemence, grandeur, and devouring fire were acceptable; nervous fits were an epidemic and even institutionalized—the fits would take place regularly twice a week on an established day and hour, thereby enabling friends of the sensitive soul to witness the performance, which would last three to four hours, with intermissions.

Smart society met at Bath and at watering spas. Gardens were landscaped in extraordinary ways, with water, ruins, and useless towers. Tea became established as a daily ritual. Masquerade dances were popular. Quizzing glasses were a typical affectation; one was to stare through them at arm's length, although drawings show them brought close to the eye. Recreations included cricket, cock fighting, and horse racing.

Women were educated to learn duty, gentleness and other virtues; they were expected to do good deeds in order to prepare them for the duties and trials of life. They strove for simplicity—Nature rather than Artfulness. They played and sang, and were permitted gentle forms of gymnastics. Ladies sank gently onto a chair and sat easily, neither relaxed nor stiff.

The other side of women's roles is revealed in this "Advice to Men" from Godey's Ladies Book, 1831:

> Be you to her virtues kind,
> To her faults be somewhat blind,
> Let her joys be unconfined
> And put your padlock on her mind.

Only lower classes went arm in arm. Servant's work became more specialized. Children stood in the presence of parents, addressed them as "sir" or "madam," and kissed their hands. They curtsied and bowed to parents, as did husbands and wives to each other.

SALUTATIONS

MAN'S BOW: Simplified from previous periods, it now consisted only of an inclination from the waist, with heels together, raising the hat with the right hand and letting the arms fall easily to the side. On straightening up, assume the elegant posture for conversing: standing in fourth position with the front knee relaxed. For a more ceremonious bow, begin with a small preliminary step to the side, bring heels together, and proceed as above.

WOMAN'S CURTSY: Step to either side, then let the free foot pass behind to fourth position. Bend the knees as the second foot moves, and take the weight onto the back leg. The body and head incline gracefully. Both knees straighten and the front, weightless, foot is brought in to join the other in a standing position.

Passing salutations were modified versions of the above. They were often done as a slight inclination of head or body and a momentary hesitation.

DANCES

As Queen of the Ballroom the *waltz* reigned from about 1815, and its elegance and grace are particularly suited to this period of languor and crinolines. There are several forms, all using the basic rhythm pattern of 1,2,3 with an accent on 1, and books of instruction give varying techniques for dancing the waltz. The form given below is that of the Viennese waltz, or turning waltz, since it is the most effective on stage and most likely to be used in choreography.

All instructions are directed to the man, who leads; the woman does the opposite, that is, his left equals her right, his forward equals her backward. Couples dance in ballroom position, the man facing the Line-of-Direction (or Line-of-Dance). This LOD is an imaginary line running clockwise around the ballroom. The man's left arm will be directed toward the center of the room.

First, balance in place while getting oriented, by (man) stepping forward with the left foot on count 1, letting the knee bend to give it an accent; then bring the right foot close in and take two small shifts of weight, right and left, on counts 2 and 3, and on the toes. In other words, down 1, up 2, up 3. now the right foot is free to step back on accented count 1, and bring the other foot close in to take two little steps in place, left, right, same as before, on counts 2 and 3. Let it flow smoothly with a down, up, up, down, up, up; keep repeating the steps; you are balancing forward and back in place. This balance step can be used along with the turning one, as below.

Quarter turns: a useful way to work up to complete turns. On each triplet make a quarter turn, rotating left. Step forward with the left foot and the first triplet ends with your facing into the center of the room; step back with the right and the second triplet ends with your facing against the LOD; after the third triplet forward you end with your back to the center of the room, and on the fourth triplet you are back to where you began.

This can be reversed so as to balance-turn rotating to the man's right, clockwise. Rotation to the right is the most usual version of the turning waltz.

The Viennese waltz is an extension of the above; instead of turning a quarter of the way around, turn half way around on each triplet. A complete turn takes two triplets, and you are alternately facing the LOD and facing away from it. Centrifugal force will help; partners should lean their upper bodies slightly away form each other—that will help the spin.

How not to get dizzy: constant turning in one direction can make the dancers dizzy. At intervals, partners stop turning and balance in place for a time. Then they can either resume turning as before or change to the other direction.

Other dances of the time: lancers, quadrille, reel, cotillion, galop.

NON-CHARACTER IMPROVISATIONS

Performing the dances will help actors become familiar with the strange clothing and comfortable with the salutations. Improvising in period will do the same, and during the process actors should keep conversation to a minimum and make no attempt to initiate dramatic action. The following situations are those of ordinary daily life.

PROMENADE AT BATH The huge central square in this fashionable resort is the site of a daily afternoon promenade. Everyone walks and talks, is there to see and be seen. Ladies in carriages stop and chat; some men are on horseback. Parasols are deployed, invitations to call are offered and accepted. One could shop, with servants to carry parcels.

AT AN ART GALLERY OPENING People arrive for the opening of an exhibition by a fashionable painter. They wander through the gallery, as much to see each other as to see the works. The painter is present, receiving his friends and admirers.

TAKING THE WATERS This is a spa for mineral waters, an indoor pavilion where various kinds of mineral waters are available for drinking. In the late morning and early afternoon, people wander about, sit, talk, periodically drink waters at small bars, visit with friends. Those bathing in the waters are carried to the baths in sedan chairs.

AT A BALL Guests enter the ballroom, mingling and greeting other guests in passing or more formally. People are seated; men find partners for the dance by bowing to the lady; she rises, curtsies, and is led to the dance space. They salute each other at the end of the dance and return to her seat or to the refreshment table, or he will bring a cooling drink to her.

CHARACTER IMPROVISATIONS

Any of the above improvisations can be played in character when the setting is appropriate. Greetings might then reflect characters' relationships or feelings—servile, cool, arrogant, sentimental, or whatever is suggested by the play.

Specific plays or scenes in work will suggest other possibilities.

Let's go dancing, you and I,
Far away from town,
And beneath October's sky,
Columbine and clown;
Autumn leaves are mad and spry,
Dancing, let us dare defy
Etiquette of town . . .

Charles Divine, "Let's Go Dancing"

VICTORIAN/ EDWARDIAN
1840 - 1910

THE TIMES

This half century saw rapid changes and great extremes. The sweetness of royal domesticity and the great Barrett-Browning romance presented vivid contrast to Darwin's opening the door to far-reaching questions on religion and science. France's politics were precarious, but her dazzling Court of the Second Empire established her as the luxury and pleasure capital of the world, a position she retained through invasion and war. The United States expanded in area and in trade, and took a civil war in her growing stride. Queen Victoria's name was given to furniture, architecture, morals, customs, and drama. Women were on the move with broader education and literary salons; Florence Nightingale helped to create the International Red Cross. Classic art was forced to allow room for the clamoring French Impressionists.

EDWARDIAN TIMES

The 1890s were the Gay 90s—*Belle Epoque* in France—a divinely decadent time in which scandalizing women wore lipstick and smoked in public, a time which adored Beardsley, Wilde, and Beerbohm for their crisp elegance, iconoclasm, and precise artificiality. In England, foremost among imperialist powers, young romantics reinvented liberty, art, and taste. Their *fin de siècle* blues were a hedonistic blend of epigrams and attitudes. The United States looked like a promised land, and her immense melting pot sucked into itself all the great, sad migration from the Irish famine and Russian pogroms, and the rest of the world's tired, homeless and poor, while remaining Anglo-Saxon in point of view and in cultural assumptions. Phonographs, electric lighting, telephones, railroads, cinemas, horseless carriages, and airplanes vied with strikes and suffragettes as pattern-changing events, and people motored, tangoed, and turkey-trotted as the world fought little wars in its preparation for World War I.

* * *

Theatre under Victoria flourished, but little of it has remained in the producing repertoire. Star vehicles, melodramas, French comedies and farces, English pantomime, and music hall offered a variety of theatre fare of no great depth. At the same time, no other period has boasted so many great actors of international stature. Opera reached a high point, and Wagner's revolutionary driving musical voluptuousness changed the sound and shape of that art.

In the decades spanning the turn of the century came the most astonishing burst of creativity in art, music, and playwriting. New ideas and influences rolled like tidal waves over every aspect of society, and in the upsurge modern theatre was born. Dramatic forms included realistic theatre, non-realistic, brittle comedies, music hall, avant-garde; the Théâtre Française guarded the classics, Antoine's Théâtre Libre initiated naturalism, and Meyerhold heralded the future. French farces, Victorian melos, meticulous realism, German expressionism, drawing room comedies, comic opera, and social drama were all offered to an avid public. Technicians were now needed, and the Ballet Russe utilized marvels of painting, sound, light, and color. An important new element was suddenly needed, and it arrived—the director.

Augustin Daly trained a couple of generations of American actors. Pathé made the first motion picture, and its development would be so rapid as to make Mary Pickford and Charlie Chaplin famous throughout the world in a few years. Wilde's comedies laughed at respectability and Gilbert and Sullivan laughed at Wilde.

On the Victorian stage: Actors Fanny Kemble, Charlotte Cushman, Rachel, J. Jefferson, the brothers Booth, Coquelin, and Bernhardt. Playwrights Turgeniev, Feydeau, Boucicault, Ibsen, Büchner, and Sardou. Composers Berlioz, Strauss, Verdi, Wagner, Offenbach, Gounod, and Bizet.

Spanning the periods: Actors Terry, Belasco, Irving, Beerbohm-Tree, Mansfield, Réjane, Duse, and Rehan; playwright Strindberg, and the Théâtre Libre.

On the Edwardian stage: Actors Stanislavski, Mrs. Fiske, Mrs. Pat Campbell, and Granville-Barker. Playwrights Pinero, Shaw, Wilde, Chekhov, Barrie, Schnitzler, Maeterlinck, Rostand, Yeats, Pirandello, Wederkind, Synge, d'Annuzio, and Gilbert and Sullivan. Directors Meyerhold, Reinhardt, and Daly; dancer Isadora Duncan, designers Appia and Craig, the Abbey Theatre, and composers Strauss and Puccini.

In the arts: Victorian artists Cruikshank, Manet, Dégas, Whistler, and writer-artist Rosetti and Morris. Writers Emerson, Hawthorne, Sand, Longfellow, Poe, Thackeray, Gautier, Dickens, Thoreau, the Brownings, Tolstoy, Melville, Flaubert, Whitman, Dostoevsky, Dumas, Verlaine, Carroll, Trollope, and Alcott. Composers Chopin, Liszt, Franck, Brahms, Moussorgsky, and Tchaikowsky.

Spanning the periods: Artists Renoir, Monet, Cezanne, and Gauguin; writers Zola, Mallarme, and France, and the composer Grieg.

In the arts: Edwardian artists Van Gogh, Toulouse-Lautrec, Matisse, Beardsley, and Picasso. Writers Colette, Conrad, Galsworthy, and Proust. Composers Mahler, Debussy, and Bartok.

THE CLOTHING

Victorian. The trend of the previous era continued: men's clothing became  more comfortable as women's fashions turned toward other countries and periods for inspiration: Greek, Renaissance, and Gothic, to which the newly invented sewing machine added an orgy of decoration. The silhouette of the time now contrasted the sexes: the wider the female outline, with crinoline and bustle, the narrower the male form, resembling the stovepipe—tall and slim in the legs, the neck, the torso, and the hat.

Man's comparatively increased comfort with looser clothes and lower coat collars was offset by luxuriant whiskers, stiff fabrics, a whaleboned stock or wrapped neckcloth. Shorter coats and sack coats were used, at first for informal or sports wear. Fitted waists faintly echoed the earlier hourglass shape. Prince Albert, the man, popularized the garment. Wide lapels, high celluloid shirt collars, low heels, and satin waistcoats with showy buttons were typical, and a great variety of overcoats was available. For the first time, approximately the same kinds of clothes were worn by professional men, business men, and civil servants, and clothing differences were now achieved by fabric, tailoring, and accessories—the sword turned into an umbrella as upper class fashion gave way to the need for managers; men opted for black as they entered offices in the new industries. Accessories could be canes, signet rings, watches on chains, gloves, monocles or pince-nez, cigars (cigarets were at first considered effete), white gloves for dancing, and hat boxes or band boxes for "bands," as shirt linen was called.

Women were demure in manners, clothes, and hair, which they wore in braids and curls. Barton describes the 1856 lady of fashion coping with long underdrawers trimmed with embroidery or lace, a couple of under petticoats, a flannel one, the principal stiff petticoat $3^{1}/_{2}$ yards around, heavily quilted to the knee and stiffened with rounds of whalebone, another petticoat with three flounces of crinoline or starched muslin, more muslin petticoats prettily decorated, which might show when the skirt was looped off the ground. All this was carefully guided and discreetly controlled, and, as before, one walked with small gliding steps so as to keep the skirt from swaying; controlled too by remaining in the center of the skirt, particularly when coming to a stop. In 1858 came the patent tilter, steel wire rounds which eliminated all but one petticoat, for the bell-shaped look. By the 1860s bustles did away with the tilter; the bulkier the bustle the more one leaned forward in compensation, giving a curved, hyper-extended line from bust to bustle. Huge balloon sleeves were popular. Accessories could be fans (see Ch. 3, p 46), handkerchiefs, parasols, long gloves, mitts, boas, jewelry, muffs, reticules. For hats they wore turbans, poke bonnets, or small hats perched high. Cloaks, shawls, and low heeled ankle boots were popular.

Edwardian.
The continuing trend toward comfort ushered in the basic modern dress consisting of shirt, trousers, coat, vest, and tie for men. Women were freed of "dress improvers" like crinolines and bustles, but not of corsets. Their silhouettes were modified into that of the princess line. A wasp waist was its exaggerated feature; in 1900 the ideal average size 36 measured 36-22-40, with many aspiring to the desired 18-inch waist (compare with today's standard pattern size of 36-28-39) achieved by tightly laced corsets. Dust ruffles enabled the lady to hold up her skirt gracefully so as to show the froth of white lace below, but she adroitly never revealed the ankle. Both sexes wore special clothes for sports, and motoring in the open cars required caps, dustcoats, veils, and goggles. Women, still corsetted, wore slightly shorter skirts for bicycling (with bloomers) and tennis; often their sports clothes were modeled on those of the men: riding suits and top hat, straw boater. And women going into the work world as teachers, typewriters (as they were called), nurses, etc., wore tailored suits of skirt and jacket, with a shirtwaist.

At the turn of the century hair was arranged in pompadours, puffs, knots, with much ornamentation. Hats were very large or very small, from tiny toques to great feathered structures. Large hats perched atop a high coiffure needed to be carefully lifted up after removing the large hatpins, placed in the lap as one methodically replaced the hatpins in the same holes. The train was favored for formal occasions, and in order to sit one approached the chair, turned in place so that the train arranged itself gently around one's feet, and

sat. To turn and walk, one walked around it. Sloping shoulders were popular, and mantillas and capes for outer wear replaced shawls. Accessories could be parasols, large fans, bouquet holders, small muffs, handkerchiefs, jewelry, reticules, gloves, caps or bonnets carried in hat boxes or band boxes, pince-nez (which could be pulled out or snapped back with a decisive click), large handbags, feather boas, and card cases; "fast" women would have cigaret holders for use in private.

Men's informal clothes included cardigans, pullovers, and blazers. On their heads they wore top hats, bowlers, straw boaters fastened to the lapel by a cord (because of the wind while boating), caps, or black, wide-brimmed felts, the last favored by artists and sometimes worn with a large, flowing tie. Facial hair varied from side whiskers to Van Dyke beards. Accessories could be tie pins, watches on chains with trinkets attached, lapel flowers, umbrella, and gloves. By 1905 they were in sack coats, waistcoats, and wide-winged stiff collars, with bow ties, knickerbockers, and Inverness capes. They wore a morning coat in the morning, a frock coat in the afternoon, a dinner jacket for dinners with no ladies present, and tailcoats for formal, mixed occasions.

Aprons advertised one's status or work: cooks wore checked gingham, waitresses and maids white bibbed aprons, school mistresses and shop girls wore black sateen, and aprons for ladies were dainty, decorated, and non-functional.

EXERCISES ON DRESS AND MOVEMENT

First, examine the drawings of the clothing; also look at costume books in the library (see the bibliography and/or your own library). Choose a picture and, working by yourself, mime actions of getting dressed in that costume, using an imaginary full length mirror. Do not be concerned with revealing character, but simply have your body know what it is "wearing."

Then find a way to stand, walk, sit, and handle small props, if any. Be guided by the pictures, and remember that the attitudes they depict were normal and natural to those people in that time.

Next, choose three pictures and copy each of the attitudes of the body in turn. Then link the three by going indirectly from one to another, without breaking the postural-gestural feeling. The challenge lies in passing from one attitude to another. Finally, if you can find a justification for the series of movements, use it and play out whatever circumstances you have invented.

EXERCISE FOR PRECISION: Oxenford states, for the 18th century, that "diction has to be precise but not affected (except in the case of fops), and the integration of speech and movement exceedingly accurately timed." The same can hold true of an elegant Edwardian style. As an exercise and drill for coordinated timing, not necessarily true for all characters or every situation on stage, take any line and say it with a corresponding move of any kind, so that the line and the gesture or movement begin and end at the same time. Do this several times, changing lines and changing movement.

CUSTOMS / MANNERS

The English upper classes were dignified and formal; a sort of conscious superiority was never far below the surface. Although propriety was all-important, it was balanced by early Victorian man's light, irreverent touch—a certain dash taken from the Regency. Strong, self-reliant Empire-builders, they swaggered confidently. They were highly protective toward ladies, except, of course, servants and light women; gentlemen opened doors for ladies (ladies first!), picked up fallen objects, stood when ladies entered or stood, etc. The hierarchy of professions was: politics, church, bar, diplomatic service, solicitor, banking, medicine, commerce—in that order.

While young girls could be gay and silly, with bouncing curls and ribbons, women were expected to be self-controlled, polite, never to show anger or be rude. Her property belonged to her husband. To run a household and oversee the care of the children, with the number of domestics carried according to the wealth and position of the master of the house, she supervised a team of servants with strictly defined specialities; Mrs. Beeton's book of household management, 1861, was much consulted.

Recreation for women included needlework with embroidery, lace, and beads; indoor gardening, mild sports such as croquet, tennis and bicycling, picnics, playing and singing, dancing, archery, and painting in water colors. Parlor elocution followed Delsarte's methods of suiting gesture to speech, and handbooks of precise instruction told one how.

Afternoon tea was a daily ritual, and dinner was served at 7 o'clock. Men seldom smoked in public and never in mixed company; after smoking in the smoking room and while wearing a smoking jacket, one was expected to change jackets and rinse the mouth before meeting ladies. A popular stance for Victorian men was that of bearing the weight on the back leg, one hand holding the lapel and the other hand behind the back. They also caressed their whiskers and stroked their moustaches.

Around 1870 handshakes replaced bows, which were now relegated to the ballroom, or upon entering a room; on formal occasions both sexes could either bow or shake hands. But to royalty one always bowed or curtsied. Ordinary salutations were simple but the etiquette governing who, when, and how remained as complex as ever. The lady was the first to recognize a male acquaintance or friend, with a slight bow of the head in the case of the first, and adding her hand to take in the case of the second if she were a married woman. The man raised his hat and held it high as he bowed, removing his cigar if any. Only if the lady offered her hand did he take it. Two ladies might shake hands gently. A superior was the first to offer the hand. If a couple was being introduced in order to dance, they exchanged salutations, not handshakes. Only family members walked arm in arm. In France, however, the older customs were retained. Bows and curtsies were the rule, and the handshake was reserved for long acquaintanceship, thus clinging to its traditional significance as a pledge of honor or friendship. Interestingly enough, today it is the French who shake hands unfailingly on all occasions, and exchange kisses on the cheeks upon most.

Hands were kissed as a gallant gesture, or out of respect or affection. Cousins, not two males, kissed on the cheek. Dowagers could gaze fearlessly, but girls were not supposed to look anyone straight in the eye. Hats, sticks, or elegant parasols could be taken into the drawing room, but not umbrellas. One never put a hat on a chair or table, but kept it in hand. On greeting ladies the man spoke to each in succession according to age or rank. On introduction to a lady he would bow, unless she offered her hand instead; with a man he shook hands. To lead a lady the man offered his arm, on which she placed her fingers.

Gentlemen did not sit stiffly on the edge of a chair, nor lounge in it. They could cross their legs. Straddling a chair or tilting it was pardonable in a bachelor's room but not in a lady's drawing room. The lady herself sank gently into a chair, upright but not stiff, her feet scarcely showing and never crossed. To display graceful arms she could slowly roll up the veil in order to drink tea.

Sports were followed seriously: cricket, billiards, football, skating, cycling, tennis, croquet, and archery. For the first soccer match, 1869, the players wore tweed suits and caps. Baseball came into being in 1871. Women eagerly engaged in sports, but were not to show any unbecoming effects such as breathing hard or appearing flushed. By the 1890s bicycling and tennis were practiced by all; there were women tennis champions as well as men. Men devoted their days either to business or sports, depending on their income, and evenings to cards or billiards, at home or in clubs.

As respectability became more important, the cultivated pose was that of a pompous, responsible smugness; the "phlegmatic Englishman" was to be upright, reliable, clean-living, religious (at least outwardly), well-bred, genteel, uninterested in intellectual pursuits, and trained to show no emotion to family or lower orders. Morality was simple: evil was always punished here, and virtue rewarded in the next world. Important activities for women were to visit the sick and poor, doing charitable works, and social visits. The Edwardians accepted broader education for women, service in military corps, and women's activities on behalf of suffrage and against child labor.

"Calling" was a firmly rooted custom, done mainly by women, and the tedium of paying endless visits was replaced by the use of calling cards, separate ones for wife and for husband. Cards were left for the lady, for the husband, and for grown children. A visit was not to exceed a quarter of an hour, so one had to keep to small talk couched in short sentences. The French had a fixed day "at home" for callers.

The turn-of-the-century Esthetes affected flowing garments, ordered disorder, and languid poses, Wilde serving as model for the "transcendental" young hero in *Patience*. They were said to delight in Oriental vases, Chinese screens, Japanese fans, sunflowers, lilies, yearning for the Infinite, knee breeches, velvet jackets, flowing ties, medieval or Renaissance dresses, and affected walking and talking. They were often laughed at, but many of their ideas embodied principles which were in revolt against the outwardly respectable, hide-bound conventions.

SALUTATIONS

Salutations remained essentially the same as in the earlier era.

WOMAN'S CURTSY: Step to either side, let the other foot pass through behind that foot to fourth position. Bend the knees as the second foot moves, and take the weight onto the back leg. The body and head incline gracefully. Shift weight back to the front foot and straighten body and knees. The back foot can be brought close to the other for standing.

MAN'S BOW: With heels together in first position, make a graceful inclination of the head and body from the waist. If one is wearing a hat, raise it with the hand furthest away from the one being greeted and let it fall gracefully to the side. Posture and attitude are characterized by an elegant simplicity. Replace the hat, if that is appropriate, after straightening up.

PASSING SALUTATIONS: These vary from perfunctory, modified versions of the above, to a simple inclination of the head in acknowledgement.

DANCES

The *waltz* (see Ch. 6 p 81 for instructions) continued to be danced all through this period.

Another ballroom favorite was the *polka*. Couples dance in ballroom position; his left arm, and her right one, are pointing along the Line-of-Direction (or Line-of-Dance). This LOD is an imaginary line going counterclockwise around the ballroom. He faces away from the center of the room.

Instructions are directed to the man, who leads; the woman does the opposite, so that his left equals her right, his forward equals her backward. With left foot (man) step to the side, along the LOD, count 1; bring the right foot close and take the weight, count 2; and another side step with the left, count 3; hold count 4 for the moment. Repeat the other way, starting with the right foot and moving to the right. The pattern is step-together-step-hold, step-together-step-hold.

Next, add the all-important little hop on the supporting leg, on the count

4 that was held; so it's step-together-step-hop. Do this back and forth in place to get the swing of it. Work up gradually to the full turns (half a turn on each hop) by shifting direction slightly on each step-together-step-hop, until you are turning continuously clockwise, to the man's right, taking two units to get around one full turn. You can stop and change direction at any time. By leaning the upper bodies slightly away from each other, the centrifugal force helps to swing the partners around in their circling.

Heel-toe polka This variation combines the turning polka with the following. Begin in the same position, left shoulder pointing along the LOD. Hopping on each step, place the left heel out to the side while hopping right, count 1; bring the left toe in to the hopping right foot, count 2; then a basic step-together-step-hop, starting left and without turning. Repeat the sequence with the right heel and toe while hopping on the left; this time you are moving back against the LOD, your heads looking over your holding arms. Do four of these heel-toe combinations, and then do eight turning polkas for the complete pattern.

Other dances of the time: lancers, quadrille, reel, galop, cotillion.

NON-CHARACTER IMPROVISATIONS

Performing the dances will help actors become familiar with the strange clothing and comfortable with the salutations. Improvising in period will do the same, and during the process actors should keep conversation to a minimum and make no attempt to initiate dramatic action. The following situations are those of ordinary daily life.

THE BOAT TRAIN Six or eight passengers arrive to take the boat train to the Channel, intending to cross to the continent. The train compartment, not commodious, has two rows of seats facing; the door gives onto the corridor and the window to the outside. Passengers find their reserved seats, rack the luggage, and compose themselves for the journey. A maid might bring her mistress some tea; someone may need to take down a bag to take out a book — small actions that don't lead to lengthy conversation.

AT AN ART GALLERY OPENING This is the opening of a new Beardsley show, and all fashionable London will be there, as much to be seen as to see the drawings, some of which are said to be very daring. Beardsley has not yet arrived but is certainly expected.

READING THE WILL A group of people gather in the lawyer's office in preparation for the reading of the will; relatives, close friends, servants, perhaps a colleague or the doctor or a representative from a charitable organization. Actors should decide who they are, and let the information be known to those who need it. Play the atmosphere of the room, the placement of chairs, grief or lack of it, wondering about the provisions of the will, and the other people there. This can end when the reading begins.

THE DUEL Two principals, two seconds, a referee, a doctor, and several ladies are gathered for this affair of honor with pistols. The atmosphere is tense and formal; everyone knows what must be done and gets on with it, for duelling is illegal but, obviously, necessary. The pistols are examined, ladies comforted, brief exchanges made. The antagonists take their places, are paced, turn, given a cue, and fire.

THE TEA TABLE The family enters to take tea. On the table are silver teapot (use actual water), silver milk jug, teaspoons, cups and saucers, sugar bowl and tongs. The hostess pours, asking each if they want milk or not, one lump or two, and the teacups are handed around. There are also small cakes and cookies on china plates or silver salvers. A servant might bring in a calling card, then usher in a visitor. One might ring for a servant to put coal on the fire, sweep the hearth, or draw the curtains. Teacups are handed around by the butler on a formal occasion, a maidservant if less so, and by the gentlemen if the occasion is quite informal.

AT THE BALL Guests enter the ballroom, mingling and greeting the others, making a salutation at the entrance but thereafter using handshakes and bows when appropriate. Guests are seated. Men can sign the ladies' program to reserve a dance; the program card is suspended on a ribbon from her wrist but men have to remember with whom they signed for which dance. They bow first to the chaperone, bow to the lady, she rises and is escorted to the dance area. When he returns her to the chaperone they salute each other, he bows again to the chaperone, and either remains or leaves. Or he will bring a cooling drink to her and the chaperone.

CHARACTER IMPROVISATIONS

Any of the above improvisations can be played in character when the setting is appropriate. Greetings might then reflect characters' relationships or feelings—servile, cool, arrogant, sentimental, or whatever is suggested by the play. Cecily and Gwendolyn might take tea, without exchanging a word. Dancers at a ball can be in love with someone not their partners.

Specific plays or scenes in work will suggest other possibilities.

THE PICNIC, rehearsed scene for two couples. For a picnic across the lake, the ladies are beautifully got up in laces and silks, flowers, ribbons, dainty shoes, light gloves. The men wear blazers and straw boaters.

The ladies think the boat is not very clean, so the men dust off the seats. One rubs the seat with her glove . . . they sigh and sit down. Stroker tries to be careful, feathering high, letting the blades drip, dipping them smoothly. The ladies do not complain, but huddle close together and wince with each stray drop of water. The men change places and the second oarsman is enthusiastic. The ladies frantically pull coats and rugs over themselves. Finally they land for lunch.

The grass is dusty. The ladies sit bolt upright on their tiny handkerchiefs, nervously watching food being handled carelessly, wine poured, etc. After lunch the men are all for chucking the used dishes and leftover food into the hamper, but the idea fills the ladies with horror; they try to find a way to wash up. The men urge them to play ball instead. By the time the dishes are somewhat clean and the food packed neatly away, it is time to go home. The return trip . . .

THE LOST TWINS

A Multi-Period Piece

PROLOGUE

Two actors, dressed identically as cave men, mime the playing of some game (ball game, archery, or...) as children. A storm (on sound track) tosses them about and separates them.

As grown men they go about looking for each other, often passing and seeing the other but without recognition. Use all the old vaudeville gags of near collision, passing back to back, double and triple takes, etc.

Finish either with a recognition scene, or each going off, still looking.

ACT I

(Taken from *The Menaechmi of Plautus*, Act I and Act II Sc. 1 and 2. Tr. by Joseph H. Drake. New York: The Macmillan Company, 1916. Adapted by Bari Rolfe)

Cast: *Peniculus*, a parasite, hanger-on to Menaechmus I
Menaechmus I, a citizen of Epidamnus
Menaechmus II (Sosicles), a citizen of Syracuse } lost twins
Erotium, a woman loved by Menaechmus I
Cylindrus, a cook, servant of Erotium
Messenio, a slave of Menaechmus Sosicles

SCENE: At Epidamnus, a Greek city in Illyria, on the east coast of the Adriatic Sea

I, 1

Enter Peniculus, *from the Forum*

PEN.   [*soliloquizes*] The boys have given me the name Peniculus [table-brush] because when I eat I sweep the table clean. Men that bind captives with chains and put shackles on fugitive slaves act very foolishly, in my opinion at least. For if a wretched man has insult added to injury, he will have a greater desire to run away or to act badly. All precautions are useless. If you wish to guard a man properly that he may not run away, you should bind him with food and drink; you can fasten a man's nose to a full table. You will easily keep him, if you bind him with that chain. These food chains are so very elastic the more you stretch them, the more tightly they bind. Therefore I am going to this man Menaechmus, to whom now for some time I have been attached. For that man does not simply feed men; he nourishes them and creates them anew; no one gives medicine better. He himself is a young man of lordly appetite, and he gives banquet fit for Ceres. He builds up such tablesful and sets such piles of dishes, that you must stand on the couch if you want anything from the top. But the door is opening; lo, I see Menaechmus himself; he is coming out of doors.

I, 2

Enter Menaechmus, *wearing his wife's mantle under his own cloak. He scolds his wife in the house.*

MEN.   If you weren't a vixen, if you weren't an idiot, if you weren't unruly and out of your head, that which you see is disagreeable to your husband you would consider disagreeable to yourself. Furthermore, if after today you act so toward me, I'll warrant you shall go as a grass-widow to your father's house. For whenever I want to go away from home you stop me, call me back, ask me where I am going, what I am going to do, what business I have, what I am going after, what I shall bring back, what I have done away from home. I have married an inspector of customs, so necessary is it for me to tell everything that I have done or am doing. Since I provide you well with maid-servants, food, clothing, money, drapery, purple, you will quit watching your husband if you are wise. And that you may not watch me to no purpose, on account of your officiousness I shall today find a woman and arrange for a dinner somewhere away from home.

PEN.   [aside] This man pretends that he is scolding his wife; he is talking at me, for if he dines away from home, he certainly is punishing me, not his wife.

MENE.   Hurra! I have at last driven my wife away from the door! It was an excellent trick, commendable, charming, and well executed. [Lifting up the cloak he exposes the mantle] I have stolen this from the vixen to my own loss; it shall be taken to my mistress. I have taken spoil from the enemy to the profit of our allies.

PEN.   [coming forward] Hey, young man! What share, pray, have I in that spoil?

MENE.   [turning away] Heavens! I have fallen into an ambuscade.

PEN.   Oh, no! Into a barricade; don't be scared.

MENE.   [turning around] Who is this?

PEN.   It's I.

MENE.   [clasping his hand] Oh my vantage! Oh my opportunity! Welcome!

PEN.   Welcome!

MENE.   You couldn't have come at a better time than this.

PEN.   That's my style. I know all the points of vantage.

MENE.   Do you want to see something tasty?

PEN.   What cook has cooked it? I shall know as soon as I see what remains, whether or not any blunder has been made.

MENE.   Tell me, have you ever seen the picture painted in fresco, where the eagle carries off Ganymede, or where Venus carries away Adonis?

PEN.   Often, but what are those pictures to me?

MENE.   Come, look at me. Do I seem at all like them?

PEN.   What's that attire of yours?

MENE.   Say that I am a very charming man.

PEN.   Where are we going to eat?

MENE.   Say just what I tell you.

PEN.   I say it, you are a most charming man.

MENE.   Don't you add something of your own to that?

PEN.   And a jolly good fellow.

MENE.   Go on.

PEN.   No, by the gods! You have a quarrel with your wife; on that account I am the more on my guard against you.

101

MenE.   There is a place where we may, without the knowledge of my wife, burn this day on its funeral pyre and hold a wake over the ashes.

PEN.   Well, come then, how soon shall I light the pyre? The day is already half dead.

MenE.   You yourself cause the delay by talking to me.

PEN.   Punch out my eye through the sole of my foot, Menaechmus, if I say a single word to you unless you order it!

MenE.   [*motioning to him*] Come here, away from the door.

PEN.   [*moves slightly*] So be it.

MenE.   Come still farther this way.

PEN.   [*moves very slightly*] All right.

MenE.   [*impatiently*] Now retreat boldly from the den of the lioness.

PEN.   But we go farther from dinner!

MenE.   This mantle shall now be carried to my dear mistress Erotium. I shall give orders that a feast be spread for her, for you, and for myself.

PEN.   Good! You have spoken to the point. Shall I knock at the door now?

MenE.   Yes, but wait a moment.

PEN.   You've put the bowl a mile away.

MenE.   Hold! By the gods, Erotium herself is coming out! Ah, the sun— isn't it completely darkened by comparison with the brilliancy of her beauty!

I, 3

Enter Erotium

ERO.   My own dear Menaechmus, welcome!

PEN.   What of me?

ERO.   [*turning away*] You don't count.

PEN.   But the same provision is made for the supernumeraries as for the soldiers.

MenE.   I arranged a contest between him and me at your house today.

ERO.   It shall be done today.

MenE.   In that contest we shall both drink. Whichever shall there be found the better warrior with the bowl is yours. Yours to decide with which one you will be tonight.

PEN.   I would we had the weapons now, for my valor pricks me to the battle.

MenE.	How I hate my wife, my darling, when I look at you!
Ero.	And yet you can't help wearing something of hers. Why this?
MenE.	Spoil for you, my rosebud, of which I despoiled my wife.
Ero.	You easily excel, as you are more excellent than any one else that courts me.
Pen.	[aside] The woman is petting him a little, which she is looking for more spoil. How he spoils her!
MenE.	Take it as your own, since you are the only living creature congenial to my taste.
Ero.	With this feeling ought true lovers to be inspired.
MenE.	I bought that for my wife last year for four minae.
Pen.	[aside] Each one gets two minae worth.
MenE.	Arrange for a dinner at your house for us three. Get some dainties at the market-place—a pork chop, or smoked ham, or hog's jowl, or something of that sort—we'll be hungry as hawks.
Ero.	Certainly, it shall be done.
MenE.	We are off for the Forum; we'll soon be back. While the meat is cooking we'll go and have a drink. Peniculus, you follow me.
Pen.	Yes, indeed, I shall certainly keep by you; I wouldn't lose you today for the wealth of the gods.

[Exeunt Menaechmus and Peniculus]

Ero.	[speaking to a slave in her house] Call my cook Cylindrus to the door quickly.

I, 4

Enter Cylindrus

Ero.	Take a basket and money. Here you have three coins. Go and buy provisions. Get enough for three, no more and no less.
Cyl.	What sort of people are these to be?
Ero.	Menaechmus, his parasite, and I.
Cyl.	Well, they make ten, for the parasite easily does duty for eight persons.
Ero.	I have named the guests; you attend to the rest.
Cyl.	At once. The things are as good as cooked. Tell the guests to go and recline on the couches.
Ero.	Return quickly. [She goes into the house]
Cyl.	I shall be back immediately.

[Exits]

II, 1

Enter Menaechmus II (Sosicles) *of Syracuse and* Messenio, *his slave*

MenS. In my opinion, Messenio, sailors have no greater pleasure than that felt on catching sight of land, when they are afar off on the deep.

Mes. There is a greater (I shall speak plainly) if on approaching you see the land that has been your home. But, I beg of you, why have we now come to Epidamnus? Are we going around all islands as the sea does?

MenS. You know very well that I seek my twin brother.

Mes. What, pray, will be the end of the search for him? This is the sixth year since we commenced it. We have sailed around Istria, Spain, Marseilles, Illyria, all the Adriatic and Magna Graecia, and all Italian countries that the sea touches. If you were hunting a needle, you would have found it long ago, I believe, if it were in existence. You are seeking a dead man among the living; for if your brother were alive, we should have found him long since.

MenS. Then I am looking for someone who can assure me of that fact, who can say that he knows that my brother is dead; otherwise I shall not give up the search so long as I live. How dear he is to my heart!

Mes. You are seeking a knot in a bulrush. Why don't we return home, unless indeed we are going to write a book of travel?

MenS. No more smart speeches, unless you want me to teach you that the matter will be arranged to please me, not you.

Mes. [*aside*] By that speech indeed I see that I am truly a slave. He could not with such distinctness have expressed more in a few words. But nevertheless I cannot refrain from speaking. [*to Menaechmus*] Listen, Menaechmus, when I look into the purse I see that we are, in truth, equipped as if for a summer's journey, for in this search for a lost brother we may lose ourselves. It is said that among the Epidamnians are revellers and hard drinkers; many sharpers and tricksters too, dwell in this city, and the courtesans are the most currency-courting in the world. The very name shows its nature, for no man comes here but says damn 'em.

MenS. I shall look out for that. Just give the purse to me.

Mes. But why, sir?

MenS.   Lest you cause me some damage in Epidamnus. You are a great lover of women, Messenio. I, on the other hand, am an irascible man, of ungovernable temper. When I have the money you cannot wrong me and I shall not get angry with you.

Mes.   All the better, sir.

II, 2

Enter Cylindrus

Cyl.   I have provided well and according to my liking. I shall set a good meal before the diners. But lo, I see Menaechmus! Woe is me, the guests are already at the door before I return from the marketing. I'll go and speak to him. Good morning, Menaechmus.

MenS.   May the gods love you, whoever you are. [to Messenio] Do you know this man who knows me?

Mes.   Most assuredly I do not.

Cyl.   Where are the other guests?

MenS.   What other guests are you asking about?

Cyl.   Your parasite.

MenS.   My parasite? [to Messenio] Certainly this fellow is insane.

Mes.   Didn't I tell you that there are very many sharpers here?

MenS.   What parasite of mine are you looking for, young man?

Cyl.   Peniculus.

MenS.   Where is my peniculus?

Mes.   [looking into his bag] Here I have your peniculus safe in the bag.

Cyl.   Menaechmus, you come back too soon to dinner. I am just returning from the marketing.

MenS.   Young man, take this money and have a sacrifice made for yourself, for surely you are perfectly daft, whoever you are, since you are impertinent to me, a stranger.

Cyl.   Your name is Menaechmus, that much I know.

MenS.   You speak as a sane man, when you call me by my name; but where did you get acquainted with me?

Cyl.   Where did I get acquainted with you, the man that has my mistress Erotium as a mistress?

MenS.   Indeed I haven't, nor do I know who you are.

CYL.   I am Cylindrus. Don't you know my name?

MenS.   Whether you are Cylindrus or Colindrus, to the devil with you. I don't know you, and I don't want to know you.

CYL.   Don't you know me, the servant who so often fills your cup when you are drinking at our house?

Mes.   Woe is me, that I have nothing with which to smash this fellow's head!

MenS.   Are you accustomed to fill the cup for me, a man who before today has never been in Epidamnus, nor seen it?

CYL.   [pointing] Don't you live in that house yonder?

MenS.   May the gods destroy those who live there!

CYL.   [aside] He is the one who is insane, he who is calling down destruction upon himself. [to Menaechmus] Do you hear, Menaechmus? Take my advice, if you are wise, and order a sacrifice for yourself with the money you offered me; in Hercules' name, you are surely not altogether sane, Menaechmus, who are calling down curses upon yourself.

MenS.   By the same Hercules, the man is a windbag and nuisance.

CYL.   [aside to the audience] He often jokes with me in that way, in case his wife should be about. [shows basket to Menaechmus] Is this enough provision for you three, or shall I provide more for you and your parasite and your mistress?

MenS.   What parasite! What mistress!

Mes.   What depravity makes you so impertinent to him?

CYL.   What business have you with me? I don't know you. I am talking with this man whom I do know.

MenS.   Surely you are mad, or a drunken fool.

CYL   You'd better go inside and recline on the couch while I put these things on to cook. I shall go and tell Erotium that you are outside, that she may invite you in rather than have you stand here before the door. [Goes in]

         The two men look at each other
         Curtain

ACT II

(Taken from *The Comedy of Errors*, Act III, by William Shakespeare. In *The Works of William Shakespeare*, London: Ward, Lock & Co., Ltd., n.d.)

Cast: *Antipholus of Ephesus* } lost twins
     Antipholus of Syracuse
     Dromio of Ephesus } their servants, lost twins
     Dromio of Syracuse
     Angelo, a goldsmith
     Balthazar, a merchant
     Luciana, sister-in-law to Antipholus of Ephesus

SCENE: Before the house of Antipholus of Ephesus.
The two sets of twins have been separated since they were children. Antipholus of Syracuse is searching for his brother, has arrived in Ephesus. Dromio of Ephesus had earlier met Antipholus of Syracuse, each mistaking the other's identity.

III, 1

Enter Antipholus E, Dromio E, Angelo, Balthazar

ANTE. Good Signior Angelo, you must excuse us all;
My wife is shrewish when I keep not hours;
Say that I linger'd with you at your shop
To see the making of her carcanet,
And that to-morrow you will bring it home.
But here's a villain that would face me down
He met me on the mart; and that I beat him,
And charged him with a thousand marks in gold;
And that I did deny my wife and house:——
Thou drunkard, thou, what didst thou mean by this?

DROME. Say what you will sir, but I know what I know:
That you beat me at the mart, I have your hand to show:
If the skin were parchment, and the blows you gave were ink,
Your own handwriting would tell you what I think.

ANTE. I think thou art an ass.

DROME. Marry, so it doth appear
By the wrongs I suffer, and the blows I bear.
I should kick, being kick'd; and being at that pass,
You would keep from my heels, and beware of an ass.

AntE. You are sad, Signior Balthazar; pray God, our cheer
     May answer my good will and your good welcome here.

Bal. I hold your dainties cheap, sir, and your welcome dear.

AntE. O, Signior Balthazar, either at flesh or fish,
     A table full of welcome makes scarce one dainty dish.

Bal. Good meat, sir, is common; that every churl affords.

AntE. And welcome more common; for that's nothing but words.

Bal. Small cheer and great welcome makes a merry feast.

AntE. Ay, to a niggardly host and more sparing guest;
     But though my cates be mean, take them in good part;
     Better cheer may you have, but not with better heart.
     But soft! My door is lock'd. Go bid them let us in.

DromE. Maud, Bridget, Marian, Cicely, Gillian, Jen'!

DromS. [within] Mome, malthorse, capon, coxcomb, idiot, patch!
     Either get thee from the door, or sit down at the hatch;
     Dost thou conjure for wenches, that thou call'st for such store,
     When one is one too many? Go, get thee from the door.

DromE. What patch is made our porter? My master stays in the street.

DromS. Let him walk from whence he came, lest he catch cold on's feet.

AntE. Who talks within there? Ho, open the door!

DromS. Right, sir: I'll tell you when, an you'll tell me wherefore.

AntE. Wherefore? For my dinner; I have not dined to-day.

DromS. Nor to-day here you must not; come again when you may.

AntE. What art thou that keep'st me out from the house I owe?

DromS. The porter for this time, sir, and my name is Dromio.

DromE. O villain! Thou hast stolen both mine office and my name!
     The one ne'er got me credit, the other mickle blame.
     If thou hadst been Dromio to-day in my place,
     Thou wouldst have changed thy face for a name, or thy name for an
          ass.

Luc. [within] What a coil is there! Dromio, who are those at the gate?

DromE. Let my master in, Luce.

Luc. Faith, no; he comes too late;
     And so tell your master.

DromE. O Lord! I must laugh!
     Have at you with a proverb: 'Shall I set in my staff?'

Luc. Have at you with a other: that's—'When? Can you tell?'

DromS. If thy name be called Luce,
        Luce, thou hast answer'd him well.

AntE.   Do you hear, you minion? You'll let us in, I hope?

Luc.   I thought to have ask'd you.

DromS. And you said no.

DromE. So, come, help; well struck! There was blow for blow.

AntE.   Thou baggage, let me in.

Luc.   Can you tell for whose sake?

DromE. Master, knock the door hard.

Luc.   Let him knock till it ache.

AntE.   You'll cry for this minion, if I beat the door down.

Luc.   What needs all that, and a pair of stocks in the town?

Adr.   [within] Who is that at the door that keeps all this noise?

DromS. By my troth, your town is troubled with unruly boys.

AntE.   Are you there, wife? You might have come before.

Adr.   Your wife, sir knave! Go get you from the door.

DromE. If you went in pain, master, this knave would go sore.

Ang.   Here is neither cheer, sir, nor welcome; we would fain have either.

Bal.   In debating which was best, we shall part with neither.

DromE. They stand at the door, master, bid them welcome hither.

AntE.   There is something in the wind, that we cannot get in.

DromE. You would say so, master, if your garments were thin.
        Your cake here is warm within; you stand here in the cold;
        It would make a man mad as a buck, to be so bought and sold.

AntE.   Go, fetch me something; I'll break ope the gate.

DromS. Break any breaking here, and I'll break your knave's pate.

DromE. A man may break a word with you, sir; and words are but wind;
        Ay, and break it in your face, so he break it not behind.

DromS. It seems thou want'st breaking; out upon thee, hind!

DromE. Here's too much 'out upon thee!' I pray thee, let me in.

DromS. Ay, when fowls have no feathers, and fish have no fin.

DromE. Well, I'll break in; go borrow me a crow.

Bal.   Have patience, sir: O let it not be so!
        Herein you war against your reputation,
        And draw within the compass of suspect
        The unviolated honour of your wife.

Once this, ——your long experience of her wisdom,
Her sober virtue, years, and modesty,
Plead on her part some cause to you unknown;
And doubt not, sir, but she will well excuse
Why at this time the doors are made against you.
Be ruled by me: depart in patience,
And let us to the Tiger all to dinner;
And, about evening, come yourself alone,
To know the reason of this strange restraint.
If by strong had you offer to break in
Now in the stirring passage of the day,
A vulgar comment will be made of it,
And that supposed by the common rout
Against your yet ungalled estimation.
That may with foul intrusion enter in,
And dwell upon your grave when you are dead;
For slander lives upon succession;
For ever housed where it get possession.

ANTE. You have prevail'd; I will depart in quiet,
And, in despite of mirth, mean to be merry.
I know a wench of excellent discourse,
Pretty and witty; wild, and yet, too gentle;
There will we dine. This woman that I mean,
My wife, ——but, I protest, without desert,,——
Hath ofentimes upbraided me withal;
To her will we to dinner. [*To Angelo*] Get you home,
And fetch the chain; by this, I know 'tis made;
Bring it, I pray you, to the Porcupine;
For there's the house; that chain will I bestow, ——
Be it for nothing but to spite my wife, ——
Upon mine hostess there; good sir, make haste;
Since mine own doors refuse to entertain me,
I'll knock elsewhere, to see if they'll disdain me.

ANG. I'll meet you at that place some hour hence.

ANTE. Do so. This jest shall cost me some expense.

[*Exeunt*]

III, 2

Enter Luciano *and* Antipholus of Syracuse

LUC. And may it be that you have quite forgot
A husband's office? Shall, Antipholus,
Even in the spring of love, thy love-springs rot?

110

Shall love, in building, grow so ruinous?
If you did wed my sister for her wealth,
Then, for her wealth's sake, use her with more kindness;
Or if you like elsewhere, do it by stealth;
Muffle your false love with some show of blindness;
Let not my sister read it in your eye;
Be not thy tongue thy own shame's orator;
Look sweet, speak fair, become disloyalty;
Apparel vice like virtue's harbinger;
Bear a fair presence, though your heart be tainted;
Teach sin the carriage of a holy saint;
Be secret-false; what need she be acquainted?
What simple thief brags of his own attaint?
'Tis double wrong, to truant with your bed
And let her read it in thy looks at board.
Shame hath a bastard fame, well managed;
Ill deeds are doubled with an evil word.
Alas, poor women! Make us but believe
Being compact of credit, that you love us.
Though others have the arm, show us the sleeve;
We in your motion turn, and you may move us.
Then, gentle brother, get you in again,
Comfort my sister, cheer her, call her wife;
'Tis holy sport, to be a little vain,
When the sweet breath of flattery conquers strife.

ANTS.   Sweet mistress—what your name is else, I know not,
Nor by what wonder you do hit of mine—
Less in your knowledge and your grace you show not
Than our earth's wonder; more than earth divine.
Teach me, dear creature, how to think and speak;
Lay open to my earthy gross conceit,
Smother'd in errors, feeble, shallow, weak,
The folded meaning of your word's deceit.
Against my soul's pure truth why labour you
To make it wander in an unknown field?
Are you a god? Would you create me new?
Transform me, then, and to your power I'll yield.
But if that I am I, then well I know
Your weeping sister is no wife of mine,
Nor to her bed no homage do I owe.
Far more, far more to you do I decline.
O, train me not, sweet mermaid, with thy note,
To drown me in thy sister's flood of tears.

Sing, siren, for thyself, and I will dote;
Spread o'er the silver waves thy golden hairs,
And as a bed I'll take thee, and there lie.
And, in that glorious supposition, think
He gains by death that hath such means to die.
Let love, being light, be drowned if she sink!

Luc.   What, are you mad, that you do reason so?

AntS.   Not mad, but mated; how I do not know.

Luc.   It is a fault that springeth from your eye.

AntS.   For gazing on your beams, fair sun, being by.

Luc.   Gaze where you should, and that will clear your sight.

AntS.   As good to wink, sweet love, as look on night.

Luc.   Why call you me love? Call my sister so.

AntS.   Thy sister's sister.

Luc.   That's my sister.

AntS.   No,
It is thyself, mine own self's better part;
Mine eye's clear eye, my dear heart's dearer heart;
My food, my fortune, and my sweet hope's aim,
My sole earth's heaven, and my heaven's claim.

Luc.   All this my sister is, or else should be.

AntS.   Call thyself sister, sweet, for I aim thee;
Thee will I love, and with thee lead my life;
Thou hast no husband yet, nor I no wife.
Give me thy hand.

Luc.   O, soft, sir! Hold you still;
I'll fetch my sister, to get her good will.

[Exit]

Enter from the house Dromio of Syracuse

AntS.   Why, now now, Dromio! Where runn'st thou so fast?

DromS.   Do you know me, sir? Am I Dromio? Am I your man?
Am I myself?

AntS.   Thou art Dromio, thou art my man, thou art thyself.

DromS.   I am an ass, I am a woman's man, and besides myself.

AntS.   What woman's man? And how besides thyself?

DromS.   Marry sir, besides myself, I am due to a woman; one that claims me,
one that haunts me, one that will have me.

ANTS. What claims lays she to thee?

DROMS. Marry sir, such claim as you would lay to your horse; and she would have me as a beast; not that, I being a beast, she would have me, but that she, being a very beastly creature, lays claim to me.

ANTS. What is she?

DROMS. A very revered body; ay, such a one as a man may not speak of, without he say, Sir-reverence. I have but lean luck in the match, and yet she is a wondrous fat marriage.

ANTS. How dost thou mean a fat marriage?

DROMS. Marry, sir, she's the kitchen-wench, and all grease; and I know not what use to put her, but to make a lamp of her, and run from her by her own light. I warrant, her rags, and the tallow in them, will burn a Poland winter; if she lives till doomsday, she'll burn a week longer than the whole world.

ANTS. What complexion is she of?

DROMS. Swart, like my shoe, but her face nothing like so clean kept; for why? She sweats; a man may go over shoes in the grime of it.

ANTS. That's a fault that water will mend.

DROMS. No, sir, 'tis in grain; Noah's flood could not do it.

ANTS. What's her name?

DROMS. Nell, sir; but her name and three quarters, that is an ell and three quarters, will not measure her from hip to hip.

ANTS. Then she bears some breadth?

DROMS. No longer from head to foot than from hip to hip; she is spherical, like a globe; I could find out countries in her.

ANTS. In what part of her body stands Ireland?

DROMS. Marry, sir, in her buttocks; I found it out by the bogs.

ANTS. And where Scotland?

DROMS. I found it by the barrenness; hard in the palm of the hand.

ANTS. Where's France?

DROMS. In her forehead; armed and reverted, making war against her heir.

ANTS. Where's England?

DROMS. I looked for the chalky cliffs, but I could find no whiteness in them; but I guess it stood in her chin, by the salt rheum that ran between France and it.

ANTS. Where Spain?

DromS. Faith, I saw it not, but I felt it hot in her breath.

AntS.   Where America, the Indies?

DromS. O, sir, upon her nose, all o'er embellished with rubies,
        carbuncles, sapphires, declining their rich aspect to the hot breath
        of Spain; who sent whole armadoes of carracks to be ballast
        at her nose.

AntS.   Where stood Belgia, the Netherlands?

DromS. O, sir, I did not look so low. To conclude, this drudge, or
        diviner, laid claim to me; called me Dromio; swore I was assured
        to her; told me what privy marks I had about me, as, the mark
        of my shoulder, the mole in my neck, the great wart on my left
        arm, that I, amazed, ran from her as a witch;
        And, I think, if my breast had not been made of faith, and my
            heart of steel,
        She had transform'd me to a curtal dog, and made me turn i' the
            wheel.

AntS.   Go hie thee presently post to the road;
        And if the wind blow any way from shore,
        I will not harbour in this town to-night.
        If any bark put forth, come to the mart,
        Where I will walk till thou return to me.
        If every one knows us, and we know none,
        'Tis time, I think, to trudge, pack, and be gone.

DromS. As from a bear a man would run for life,
        So fly I from her that would be my wife.

                                                              [Exit]

AntS.   There's none but witches do inhabit here,
        And therefore 'tis high time that I were hence.
        She that doth call me husband, even my soul
        Doth for a wife abhor; but her fair sister,
        Possess'd with such a gentle sovereign grace
        Of such enchanting presence and discourse,
        Hath almost made me traitor to myself.
        But, lest myself be guilty to self-wrong,
        I'll stop mine ears against the mermaid's song.

                Enter Angelo *with the chain*

ANG.   Master Antipholus?

AntS.   Ay, that's my name.

ANG.   I know it well, sir. Lo, here is the chain.
        I thought to have ta'en you at the Porcupine;
        The chain unfinish'd made me stay thus long.

ANTS.   What is your will that I shall do with this?

ANG.   What please yourself, sir: I have made it for you.

ANTS.   Made it for me, sir! I bespoke it not.

ANG.   Not once, nor twice, but twenty times you have;
So home with it, and please your wife withal;
And soon at supper-time I'll visit you,
And then receive my money for the chain.

ANTS.   I pray you, sir, receive the money now,
For fear you ne'er see chain nor money more.

ANG.   You are a merry man, sir; fare you well.

[Exit]

ANTS.   What I should think of this I cannot tell;
But this I think, there's no man is so vain
That would refuse so fair an offer'd chain.
I see a man here needs not live by shifts,
When in the streets he meets such golden gifts.
I'll to the mart, and there for Dromio stay,
If any ship put out, then straight away.

[Exit]

ACT III

(Taken from *Les Menechmes ou les Jumeaux*, Act III, by Jean François Regnard, 1705. In *Théâtre Choisi de Regnard v. II*. Paris: Bibliothèque Larousse, Trans. by Bari Rolfe)

Cast: *Sir Menachmus*
  Menachmus, from the country
  Valentine, servant to *Sir Menachmus,* then also to *Menachmus*
  Isabel
  Demophon, her father
  Araminta, sister of Demophon
  Clothing merchant

SCENE: In a street
Menachmus, dressed in mourning for his just-deceased uncle who raised him, has come to the city for his inheritance and to find Isabel, his arranged bride. Through letters accidentally fallen into his hands, his lost twin, Sir Menachmus, learns of his brother's presence in the city, of the inheritance, and the plan to marry Isabel.

III, 1

    Enter Sir Menachmus, *dressed in mourning for deception purposes, and* Valentine

VAL. Your resemblance to your twin surpasses belief. You and he are identical, both now being dressed in mourning. There is no one whom you can't deceive, for even I, your valet, scarcely know you. So that I make no mistake, permit me to attach to you some sign— give me your hat.

SIR MEN. What do you mean to do?

VAL. *[placing a mark on the hat]* Mark you with a sign.

SIR MEN. The notary has already been taken in. He received me immediately with kindly welcome, and in an hour he is to pay me the inheritance.

VAL. He's about to pay you the whole amount, 60,000 ecus?

SIR MEN. 60,000 ecus.

VAL. An honest man! But others have already mistaken your twin for you. Araminta, thinking he was you, wanted to take him off to dine with her. Surprised, bewildered, knowing not what to say,

	thinking that she was setting some sort of trap, he dealt with her brusquely and they quarreled. If I hadn't calmed them down, it would have gone badly for him.
SIR MEN.	But hasn't he the least suspicion about me?
VAL.	What suspicion could he possibly have? For twenty years he thought you all too dead; never would he imagine you to be alive, and in this very town.
SIR MEN.	The adventure is amusing, and we'll have a good laugh. Now let's go and see the future father-in-law and bride-to-be. [Valentine knocks at Demophon's door, who comes out]

III, 2

VAL.	Have I the honor to address M. Demophon?
DEM.	Thus am I called.
VAL.	I am most delighted to have found you. Here is my master, Sir Menachmus, just arrived from Peronne, as arranged, in order to marry your charming daughter.
DEM.	Ah [bowing] Sir, allow me to embrace you to demonstrate my great happiness [does so].
SIR MEN.	[Bows, then embraces him] My own embrace, sir, reveals my similar joy. All due respect is hereby rendered you as owed to a father-in-law.
DEM.	Your appearance, your air, your spirit all enchant me; and my heart would be utterly content if your deceased uncle, my dear friend, were yet alive to see this alliance.
SIR MEN.	Ah, sir, you recall from his ashes an uncle whom I loved most tenderly. This boy will tell you how much I sorrowed on his death, how many tears I shed.
VAL.	May Heaven rest his soul! To speak of him is to touch a painful chord . . . But he was pretty old.
DEM.	Old! We were both the same age, around fifty.
VAL.	That word could be understood in several ways, according to how one takes it. I say he was old for his lack of health; he complained always of some infirmity.
DEM.	Not at all! I think that in all his life he was never ill save for the malady that caused his death.
SIR MEN.	His was a body of iron.
VAL.	True . . . however . . .
SIR MEN.	[low to Valentine] Be quiet.

DEM.	This discourse could reopen your wound. Let us take up a happier matter. You will meet my daughter, and I venture to say that her face and figure will please you.
SIR MEN.	In truth, I count very little upon my merits, and more upon her filial duty.
DEM.	You are highly mistaken, you do yourself injustice. From her first glance she should be enchanted. Besides, Isabel is soft putty that I mold and shape as I wish. Should you not be her heart's desire (which would very much mistake me), she as my daughter defers to my word. Stay aside; I will call her, and you will see her without being seen.

[He goes into his house]

III, 3

SIR MEN.	Leave me here; go and find my brother. Above all, keep him from going to the notary for the inheritance—that's of the greatest importance.
VAL.	I will do so. But what I cannot do, given his ardent transports, is prevent him from coming here to see his mistress. So in my opinion, whatever ardor presses you, you should hold short amorous discourse.
SIR MEN.	Go quickly, I'll be here only a moment.

III, 4

Demophone *returns, followed by* Isabel.

DEM.	Isabel, come here.
ISA.	What would you, father?
DEM.	To give you good news, daughter. A gentleman from the provinces, a good match in spite of that, wishes to marry you. He should arrive at any moment.
ISA.	[aside] What do I hear? [Ed. note: she has met, and liked, Sir Menachmus; thinks this is someone else]
DEM.	This person is most suitable for you. Birth, property, all is agreeable to me. And his person will also be to your taste.
ISA.	[thinking rapidly] Dear father, please go no further. Allow me to say, with deference and with no lack of obedience, that I intend never to marry.
DEM.	What? Whence this sudden anitpathy for marriage? You have never until now employed such language.

118

ISA.	True, but after all, wisdom comes with age. Today, husbands are for the most part faithless or jealous. They want a wife to suit their whims. The most perfect husbands are those with only a few vices.
DEM.	This one will please you when you know him.
ISA.	Whoever he is, I abhor him now. It is enough that he is from the provinces. Nor would I be willing were he even a prince.
SIR MEN.	[*showing himself*] Madame, it is not necessary to rage thus against this unhappy suitor for your hand. If you do hate him, he perhaps should look elsewhere for sentiments different from your own.
ISA.	[*aside*] What do I see! It is he! It is Menachmus! My own! My lover!
DEM.	[*to Sir Menachmus*] I am in despair that a headstrong aversion should have rendered her so contrary to my wish. But I will oblige her, if you desire . . .
SIR MEN.	No, we will not oppose in any way, sir, her wishes. I would sooner die than to oblige madame to do anything that runs counter to her heart.
DEM.	Just consider the match that was destined for you: a husband so handsome, a well-born youth whose character is at least equal to his birth.
SIR MEN.	I was wrong to pitch my hopes so high.
ISA.	[*thinking rapidly*] To tell you the truth, since I have seen him my heart is no longer so firmly opposed.
DEM.	You see what a father's authority can do.
SIR MEN.	You no longer harbor that intense disdain? And your eye may, without disgust, accustom itself to sight of me?
ISA.	[*submissive*] My father requires it, and I follow my duty.

III, 5

Araminta *enters*

ARA.	[*to Sir Menachmus*] Ah! So here you are, traitor! With what impudence, after your base treatment of me, do you dare to remain so calm in my presence! Do you not fear the fury of my bruiséd heart?
SIR MEN.	[*looking about*] Madame, I don't know what you mean; this tirade is bewildering. You take me, I think, for another. On what grounds do you complain of me?
ARA.	You pretend ignorance, you two-faced, treacherous soul! You abused me, alas, with sham tenderness, and I in good faith gave you my heart without knowing yours in all its foulness.

119

SIR MEN. Truly, you honor me beyond my merits. But I understand absolutely nothing of what you say.

DEM. My word, nor I. But tell me, sister, what are you driving at? What strange humor seizes you?

SIR MEN. [to Demophon] Madame is your sister?

DEM. Yes, sir, my older sister, with whom I am angry that she lacks the sense of her years. [to her] What new caprice, what devil, I say, forces you to come here making mischief? To scandalize this gentleman who, in all his life, has neither seen nor known you, nor wishes to?

ARA. Not seen me! Not known me! It is you who are mad. For over two years this ingrate lived by my rule. He has made of my goods, good use. I provided at my expense his company accoutrements. For if I had not pitied his misfortunes he would, with all his men, have campaigned on foot!

DEM. [low to Sir Menachmus] I must tell you that she is a bit mad.

SIR MEN. [low to Demophon] She rather affects it. [aloud] I can no longer endure these accusations. Madame, I now leave your company [bows mockingly]. [low to Demophon] I'll return as soon as she has gone. [aloud] Sir, permit me to take my leave [bows to others].

DEM. [low, to him] Do not take her seriously, she has a bizarre spirit.

[Sir Menachmus leaves]

ARA. Don't think to escape me!

III, 6

ARA. I know your designs. You would like, both of you, to snatch him from me. But I'll marry him despite the daughter, the father, the uncle, the whole family; in spite of himself, and of myself too!
[she leaves]

III, 7

DEM. What strange illusions she harbors! I feel sorry for her.

ISA. I am sorry to say it, but often I am ashamed for her.

DEM. I fear that my poor sister, with her gruff temper and foolish fantasies, will create some further embarrassments.

Enter Valentine *and* Menachmus

VAL. Yes, sir, here they are, the daughter with the father. You can discuss your business with them.

DEM. [*taking Menachmus for Sir Menachmus*] Sir, for my sister and for her visions, we must ask your pardon, my daughter and I. You understand that women—and girls—are often given to wrong-headed ideas. I'm delighted that you returned so promptly.

MEN. [*puzzled, but he bows and recites as if by rote*] I offer you good day; for I, eminently suitable suitor, have come to wed a girl named Isabel, whose father you are, they say. In a few words, that's what brings me here.

DEM. [*puzzled*] I repeat what I've already said, that this match pleases me greatly. My daughter is happy; she now satisfies both love and duty. She felt at first a slight repugnance, but seeing you, her heart lost all resistance.

MEN. [*pause*] Seeing me?

DEM. Yes, of course.

MEN. [*pause*] Have we seen each other before?

DEM. You only just now left us, and seemed fair content.

MEN. [*pause*] I? I just left her?

DEM. Yes of course, you, yourself, just now. We had cheerfully made our arrangements when my sister came, and with her stupid remarks interrupted the course of our conversation. Is it possible you have already forgotten?

MEN. One of us is dreaming, you or I! You want me to believe that I've seen your daughter? When? How? Where?

DEM. Just now, right here.

MEN. It is you who are dreaming. This beginning, frankly, hardly pleases me, but whether it's the first or second time, it matters very little for our marriage.

DEM. [*aside*] This man appeared earlier to be more sensible.

MEN. Madame, [*she curtsies, he does not bow*] in letters they spoke highly of your charms, and I'm quite happy to confirm them. But I attach little importance to charms if the mind is not on par with them. I hope you will convince me of your good sense. I will state my opinion when you have spoken.

ISA. [*aside*] I no longer know him, his mind has become troubled.

MEN.   I like men of intellect more than anyone in France. I have one of
the keenest minds, and all without learning. For I find that study is
the perfect means of spoiling one's youth, and is useful for nothing.
Thus I have never stuck my nose in a book. When a gentleman, on
starting out in life, knows how to shoot, drink, and sign his name,
he is as wise as Solomon.

DEM.   Will you offer your services at Court, or in the Army?

MEN.   My mind in that choice is undeterminate. Court might have for me
a strong attraction if the subservience wouldn't bore me. On the
other hand, war has a definite appeal, but certain well-known
astrologers have assured me that I will live for one hundred years.
So, since soldiers rarely attain that age, and even though my name
could become known throughout Europe, I prefer, if I can, to fulfill
my horoscope.

VAL.   You are quite sensible.

ISA.   [low] What a boor! Can it really be him?

MEN.   Young lady, what ails you, if you please? You seem surprised, as
though I said something foolish. You have the air, I must tell you
frankly, of paying little attention to the lessons of a husband.

ISA.   I know the duties of a wife.

MEN.   I take you to be virtuous and well behaved. However, that roguish
look bodes ill; I adduce from it, without being a philosopher, that
you are capable of mischief. I beg your pardon? You wanted to
say . . . ?

DEM.   Sir, be not concerned. Isabel always has acted properly.

ISA.   Heavens! Must I listen to such . . . ? Father, allow me to leave you.
Monsieur flatters me too much; his tender compliments precisely
reveals his feelings.

[She barely curtsies, and leaves]

III, 9

DEM.   [aside] In the beginning my son-in-law had better manners . . .

MEN.   Girls do not like men who are sincere.

VAL.   You don't flatter them overmuch.

MEN.   Oh indeed no! I'm utterly frank. Wife, mistress, friend, doesn't
matter to me. I don't refrain from saying what I think.

DEM.   Ohhh, well done! You will, I hope, have the kindness to lodge
with us?

MEN.   I ought to accept the favor, but . . .

122

DEM.   How can I let you stay in a hotel? That would be such a snub . . .

MEN.   Allow me, so please you, to live at liberty for the time remaining.

DEM.   So be it. I shall arrange for the wedding. [aside] My future son-in-law seems rather unsociable. But the goods he brings are a great advantage.

                                        [He bows, and leaves]

III, 10

MEN.   Have I now seen the object whose husband I'll be?

VAL.   Yes, sir, that was the lady.

MEN.   Frankly, what do you think?

VAL.   Well, if you wish me to speak openly of her perfections, I was not exactly taken with her.

MEN.   My faith, nor I.

III, 11

VAL.   [aside, seeing someone approach] What a surplus of troubles! One of our creditors is headed this way; the clothing merchant has come to visit.

MER.   [to Menachmus, taking him for Sir Menachmus] I have this morning, sir, learned of your return, and I come, one of the first, to bid you welcome. Thus of my small duty do I humbly acquit myself. We all were concerned over your absence—I, my daughter, my wife—we trembled for fear that some misfortune overtook you.

MEN.   To be so concerned, never having ever seen me! What good souls! I would never believe to be so well loved by strangers!

MER.   We owe it to you, Monsieur, for more than one reason. You have long been a friend of my house.

MEN.   [low, to Valentine] Who is that man?

VAL.   [low, to Menachmus] He is known here as a kind of fool, a harmless character, who deludes himself that everyone he sees is one of his debtors. It is his innocent folly; he approaches everyone with a bill in hand, and I am not astonished that he has paid you some stupid compliments.

MEN.   [low, to Valentine] His folly is certainly a rare and novel one.

MER.   I am delighted to find you in good health, more than you know. Here is a certain bill that I drew up before your departure, and that you will pay, I believe, without question.

VAL.   [low, to Menachmus] What did I tell you?

MER.   For I have, during your absence, obtained a certain judgment against you. And jail order.

MEN.   And jail order?

MER.   But, benign creditor that I am, I postponed charging a bailiff with pursuits and with serving writs, for he might have hurt you.

MEN.   You really are too good, and too honest! What is your name?

MER.   Oh you know it very well.

MEN.   I'll be a rogue if I ever saw you before.

MER.   Could you forget . . .

VAL.   [taking Merchant aside] Have you not heard of his illness?

MER.   [to Valentine] No, truly, I know nothing about it.

VAL.   [to Merchant] His memory is gone; he remembers nothing, neither of what he did, nor the people he saw. So speak to him of the past is foolish. His name, even his name he often forgets.

MER.   [aside to Valentine] Heavens! What are you saying? What an unhappy event! And how comes it that at his age . . .

VAL.   [low] How? During the war he was assigned to a gun battery site from which the cannon roared with such fury that it set up a commotion in his head that interferes with the action of his memory. The too soft membrane of his weak brain . . . Oh one cannot understand the effect of cannon!

MER.   [to Menachmus] I truly pity you the misfortune that befell you. But I can assure you that the sum is truly due me, as you know.

MEN.   Yes I know, I doubt it not at all. And I know too that your own mind is disordered.

MER.   Sir, remember that these are the uniforms that I provided to your regiment last year.

MEN.   My regiment, to me! Look elsewhere to your debts; I don't have time to listen to your nonsense. You're an old fool.

MER.   I am a clothing merchant, and a church warden. If you by ill chance have lost your memory, the articles are all contained in the bill [gives him the bill].

MEN.   Well, here is your bill and how I pay it. [Tears it up and throws the pieces at the Merchant]

VAL.   [to Menachmus] Ah Monsieur, don't be angry with a crazy man.

MER.   [gathering up the pieces] Tear up a bill! Throw it in one's face! You are a rogue!

MEN.   A rogue, you say?

124

VAL.	[*throws himself between them*] Please, I beg you . . .
MER.	I'll soon show you . . .
VAL.	. . . not to make all this noise. Pity rather the stage to which Fate has reduced him.
MER.	. . . a lost memory!
VAL.	[*to Merchant*] Don't do any more business with him.
MER.	It's a horrible crime and deserves the galleys.
MEN.	[*to Valentine*] Let me cut off his nose!
VAL.	[*to Menachmus*] Let it go. What would you do, sir, with the nose of a church warden?
MER.	I want to be paid—I care nothing for the rest.
VAL.	[*to Merchant*] Leave, sir, please leave. You will be the cause of a fatal accident.
MER.	Yes, I'll leave, but perhaps before an hour passes I'll make him change his tune—and his dwelling place! Your servant sir!

[*Exits*]

III, 12

VAL.	Why get upset with a fool?
MEN.	What made him come here to make me the target of his impertinences? Let him find another place for his extravagances. Let's go to my notary, and not delay longer.
VAL.	Later, sir, we'll waste our time; he is not at home, but should soon return there. In a little while I'll be back to get you, and take you to him. Certain pressing duty calls me elsewhere.
MEN.	Then I'll wait for you. Go on, hurry up. I'll walk for a moment to calm my anger. Everyone is crazy, I think, in this town. My faith, of all the people I've seen today, I've found only myself reasonable, and you.

[*Exits*]

III, 13

VAL.	I mean to watch his every move, as the fish enters in our wicker trap. All is as successful as we would wish; and I hope this very day to serve both Love and Fortune!

ACT IV

(Taken from *The Importance of Being Earnest,* Act II of the original four-act version. London: Methuen & Co., Ltd., 1957)

Cast: *Jack Worthing,* called Ernest Worthing in the city
      Algernon Moncrief, called Ernest Worthing in the country
      Merriman, servant
      Gribsby, solicitor
      Dr. Chasuble
      Miss Prism
      Cecily, niece to Jack Worthing

SCENE: In the garden
This is not, of course, a story of lost twins, but of mistaken identity. Jack and Algernon, each in turn, have passed themselves off as Ernest. At this moment Algernon, as Ernest, is visiting at Jack's home, and paying court to Cecily Cardew.

II

Jack, Algernon, Cecily, Chasuble *and* Prism *in the garden; Merriman enters.*

MER.   [*to Algernon*] I beg your pardon, sir, there is an elderly gentleman wishes to see you. He has just come in a cab from the station. [*Hands card on salver*]

ALG.   To see me?

MER.   Yes sir.

ALG.   [*reads card*] Parker and Gribsby, Solicitors. I don't know anything about them. Who are they?

JACK   [*takes card*] Parker and Gribsby. I wonder who they can be. I expect, Ernest, they have come about some business for your friend Bunbury. Perhaps Bunbury wants to make his will and wishes you to be executor. [*To Merriman*] Show the gentleman in at once.

MER.   Very good, sir.

                                                    [*Exits*]

JACK   I hope, Ernest, that I may rely on the statement you made to me last week when I finally settled all your bills for you. I hope you have no outstanding accounts of any kind.

ALG.   I haven't any debts at all, dear Jack. Thanks to your generosity, I don't owe a penny, except for a few neckties, I believe.

JACK	I am sincerely glad to hear it.
MER.	[*entering with caller*] Mr. Gribsby.

[Exits]

GRIB.	[*to Dr. Chasuble*] Mr. Ernest Worthing?
MISS P.	This is Mr. Ernest Worthing.
GRIB.	Mr. Ernest Worthing?
ALG.	Yes.
GRIB.	Of B4, The Albany?
ALG.	Yes, that is my address.
GRIB.	I am very sorry, sir, but we have a writ of attachment for 20 days against you at the suit of the Savoy Hotel Co. Ltd. for £762 14s 2d.
ALG.	Against me?
GRIB.	Yes, sir.
ALG.	What perfect nonsense! I never dine at the Savoy at my own expense. I always dine at Willis's. It is far more expensive. I don't owe a penny to the Savoy.
GRIB.	The writ is marked as having been served on you personally at The Albany on May the 27th. Judgment was given in default against you the fifth of June. Since then we have written to you no less than fifteen times, without receiving any reply. In the interest of our clients we had no option but to obtain an order for committal of your person.
ALG.	Committal! What on earth do you mean by committal! I haven't the smallest intention of going away. I am staying here for a week. I am staying with my brother. If you imagine I am going up to town the moment I arrive you are extremely mistaken.
GRIB.	I am merely a solicitor myself. I do not employ personal violence of any kind. The Officer of the Court, whose function it is to seize the person of the debtor, is waiting in the fly outside. He has considerable experience in these matters. That is why we always employ him. But no doubt you will prefer to pay the bill.
ALG.	Pay it? How on earth am I going to do that? You don't suppose I have got any money? How perfectly silly you are. No gentleman ever has any money.
GRIB.	My experience is that it is usually relations who pay.
ALG.	Jack, you really must settle this bill.
JACK	Kindly allow me to see the particular items, Mr. Gribsby . . . [*turns over immense folio*] . . . £762 14s 2d since last October. I am bound to say I never saw such reckless extravagance in all my life. [*Hands it to Dr. Chasuble*]

Miss P.	£762 for eating! There can be little good in any young man who eats so much, and so often.
Dr.C	We are far away from Wordsworth's plain living and high thinking.
Jack	Now, Dr. Chasuble, do you consider that I am in any way called upon to pay this monstrous account for my brother?
Dr.C	I am bound to say that I do not think so. It would be encouraging his profligacy.
Miss P.	As a man sows, so let him reap. This proposed incarceration might be most salutary. It is to be regretted that it is only for 20 days.
Jack	I am quite of your opinion.
Alg.	My dear fellow, how ridiculous you are! You know perfectly well that the bill is really yours.
Jack	Mine?
Alg.	Yes, and you know it is.
Dr.C	Mr. Worthing, if this is a jest, it is out of place.
Miss P.	It is gross effrontery. Just what I expected from him.
Cec.	And it is ingratitude. I didn't expect that.
Jack	Never mind what he says. This is the way he always goes on. You mean to say now that you are not Ernest Worthing, residing at B4, The Albany? I wonder, as you are at it, that you don't deny being my brother at all. Why don't you?
Alg.	Oh! I am not going to do that, my dear fellow. It would be absurd. Of course I'm your brother. And that is why you should pay this bill for me.
Jack	I will tell you quite candidly that I have not the smallest intention of doing anything of the kind. Dr. Chasuble, the worthy Rector of this parish, and Miss Prism, in whose admirable and sound judgment I place great reliance, are both of the opinion that incarceration would do you a great deal of good. And I think so, too.
Grib.	[*pulls out watch*] I am sorry to disturb this pleasant family meeting, but time passes. We have to be at Holloway not later than four o'clock; otherwise it is difficult to obtain admission. The rules are very strict.
Alg.	Holloway!
Grib.	It is at Holloway that detentions of this character take place always.
Alg.	Well, I really am not going to be imprisoned in the suburbs for having dined in the West End.
Grib.	The bill is for suppers, not for dinners,

ALG.   I really don't care. All I say is that I am not going to be imprisoned in the suburbs.

GRIB.   The surroundings I admit are middle class; but the goal itself is fashionable and well-aired; and there are ample opportunities of taking exercise at certain stated hours of the day. In the case of a medical certificate, which is always easy to obtain, the hours can be extended.

ALG.   Exercise! Good God! No gentleman ever takes exercise. You don't seem to understand what a gentleman is.

GRIB.   I have met so many of them, sir, that I am afraid I don't. There are the most curious varieties of them. The result of cultivation, no doubt. Will you kindly come now, sir, if it will not be inconvenient to you.

ALG.   [*appealingly*] Jack!

MISS P.   Pray be firm, Mr. Worthing.

DR. C   This is an occasion on which any weakness would be out of place. It would be a form of self-deception.

JACK   I am quite firm, and I don't know what weakness or deception of any kind is.

CEC.   Uncle Jack! I think you have a little money of mine, haven't you? Let me pay this bill. I wouldn't like your own brother to be in prison.

JACK   Oh! I couldn't possibly let you pay it, Cecily. That would be absurd.

CEC.   Then *you* will, won't you? I think you would be sorry if you thought your own brother was shut up. Of course, I am quite disappointed with him.

JACK   You won't speak to him again, Cecily, will you?

CEC.   Certainly not, unless, of course, he speaks to me first. It would be very rude not to answer him.

JACK   Well, I'll take care he doesn't speak to you. I'll take care he doesn't speak to anybody in this house. The man should be cut. Mr. Gribsby...

GRIB.   Yes, sir.

JACK   I'll pay this bill for my brother. It is the last bill I shall ever pay for him, too. How much is it?

GRIB.   £762 14s 2d. Ah! The cab will be five-and-ninepence extra; hired for the convenience of the client.

JACK   All right.

MISS P.   I must say that I think such generosity quite foolish.

129

DR.C   [with a wave of his hand] The heart has its wisdom as well as the head, Miss Prism.

JACK   Payable to Parker and Gribsby, I suppose?

GRIB.   Yes, sir. Kindly don't cross the cheque. Thank you. [To Dr. Chasuble] Good day. [Dr. Chasuble bows coldly] Good day. [Miss Prism bows coldly] [To Algernon] I hope I shall have the pleasure of meeting you again.

ALG.   I sincerely hope not. What ideas you have for the sort of society a gentleman wants to mix in. No gentleman ever wants to know a solicitor who wants to imprison one in the suburbs.

GRIB.   Quite so, quite so.

ALG.   By the way, Gribsby: Gribsby, you are not to go back to the station in that cab. That is my cab. It was taken for my convenience. You have got to walk to the station. And a very good thing, too, Solicitors don't walk nearly enough. I don't know any solicitor who takes sufficient exercise. As a rule they sit in stuffy offices all day long neglecting their business.

JACK   You can take the cab, Mr. Gribsby.

GRIB.   Thank you, sir.

                                                                    [Exits]

CEC.   The day is getting very sultry, isn't it, Dr. Chasuble?

DR.C.   There is thunder in the air.

MISS P. The atmosphere requires to be cleared.

DR.C.   Have you read the *Times* this morning, Mr. Worthing? There is a very interesting article on the growth of religious feeling among the laity.

JACK   I am keeping it for after dinner.

MER.   [enters] Luncheon is on the table, sir.

ALG.   Ah! That is good news. I am excessively hungry.

CEC.   But you have lunched already.

JACK   Lunched already?

CEC.   Yes, Uncle Jack. He had some pate de foie gras sandwiches, and a small bottle of that champagne that your doctor ordered for you.

JACK   My '74 champagne!

CEC.   Yes, I thought you would like him to have the same one as yourself.

JACK   Oh! Well, if he has lunched once, he can't be expected to lunch twice. It would be absurd.

Miss P.	To partake of two luncheons in one day would not be liberty. It would be licence.
Dr.C.	Even the pagan philosophers condemned excess in eating. Aristotle speaks of it with severity. He uses the same terms about it as he does about usury.
Jack	Doctor, will you escort the ladies into luncheon?
Dr.C.	With pleasure.

[*They go into the house*]

Jack	Your Bunburying hs not been a great success after all. Algy. I don't think it is a good day for Bunburying, myself.
Alg.	Oh! There are ups and downs in Bunburying, just as there are in everything else. I'd be all right if you would let me have some lunch. The main thing is that I have seen Cecily and she is a darling.
Jack	You are not to talk of Miss Cardew like that. And you are not going to have any luncheon. You have lunched already.
Alg.	I only had some chanpagne and one or two sandwiches.
Jack	Yes, my champagne and one or two of my sandwiches.
Alg.	Well, I don't like your clothes. You look perfectly ridiculous in them. There is no use in being in mourning for me any longer. I have never been in better health than I am in at the present moment. Why on earth don't you go up and change? It is perfectly childish to be in deep mourning for a man who is actually staying for a whole week with you in your house as a guest.
Jack	You are certainly not staying with me for a whole week as a guest or anything else. You have got to leave.
Alg.	I certainly won't leave you so long as you are in mourning. It would be most unfriendly. If I were in mourning you would stay with me, I suppose. I should think it very unkind if you didn't.
Jack	Well, will you go if I change my clothes?
Alg.	Yes, if you are not too long. I never saw anybody take so long to dress, and with such little result.
Jack	Well, at any rate, that is better than being always over-dressed as you are.
Alg.	If I am occasionally a little over-dressed, I make up for it by being always immensely over-educated.

131

JACK   Your vanity is ridiculous, your conduct an outrage, and your presence in my garden utterly absurd. However, you have got to catch the three-fifty, and I hope you will have a pleasant journey back to town. This Bunburying, as you call it, has not been a great success for you.

                                                                    [*Exits*]

ALG.   I think it has been a great success. I'm in love with Cecily, and that is everything. It is all very well, but one can't Bunbury when one is hungry. I think I'll join them at lunch.

ACT V

(Recognition scene by Bari Rolfe)

Cast: *Morley Similus*, marine shipping agent
Adrienne, his wife
Lester Similus, on vacation
Humphrey, his secretary

SCENE: A street in Venice, California

> Humphrey *crosses briskly from SL to SR; stops dead at SR wings*
> *staring off. He quickly does a take or two to SL, back to SR as*
> *though not believing his eyes*

HUM.   Wha... who... wh... can't be... hey... how did... Mr. S,
how did you get... Why, I just saw you back there at the wharf
cafe... you couldn't... you're having coffee HERE —I mean—
you're having coffee THERE, with some woman...

LES.   [*from off SL*] Stop mumbling and bumbling, you idiot. What are
you going on about?

HUM.   I tell you, Mr. S, I just this minute left you over there, I turn around
and here you are...

LES.   You're daft! I've been sitting here for over an hour. You saw someone else.

HUM.   I tell you it was you! Or someone who could pass for you! Look, I'll
show you—just come along. He's right here, I'll show you I'm not
dreaming—come on— [*as Lester emerges from SL wings*] see for
yourself...

LES.   Okay, okay, it's a nice walk on a nice day...

> [*They continue the dialogue facing each other as Humphrey slowly draws*
> *his employer toward DR. When Humphrey is near SC, Adrienne enters*
> *from SR followed by Morley Similus. She is berating him and turns back*
> *and forth continuously as she leads toward SC. He is placating*]

ADR.   I'm up to here with this business of either who-are-you-lady or else
my-dear-wife. [*He expostulates "My dear of course you're..." but*
she pays no attention] I tell you Simi—or shall I call you [*elaborately*]
Mr. Morley Similus—one minute you don't know me, the next
minute you do. And I'm tired of this charade...

> [*The two dialogues continue at the same time. When Humphrey and*
> *Adrienne, backs toward each other, are at SC, the twins, who see each*

133

other, stop. Their companions, unseeing, continue to move until each has passed the other twin, shifting in direction to accommodate to the gag.

Each one turns, sees the back of the one they take for their companion; they exasperatedly go to them to turn them around, still harangueing. The twins are dazed, uncomprehending, let themselves be turned away but twist to look back at each other. They make ineffectual attempts —"Hey, wait a sec . . . do you see . . . lemme . . ."

Adrienne and Humphrey now catch sight of the other, their own, twin; thinking they've fastened on a stranger —"Oops, excuse . . .", they start toward the other twin, stop, do double takes and, astonished, fade into silence, watching fascinated from US during the ensuing exchange. The twins stare at each other]

LES.	*[pause]* Hi.
MOR.	*[pause]* 'Lo.

[They examine each other]

LES.	*[pause]* My name's Similus *[offers hand]*.
MOR.	*[pause]* My name's Similus *[takes hand]*.
LES.	*[pause]* I'm from Syracuse, New York.
MOR.	*[pause] I'm* from Syracuse, New York. Or once was.

[By coincidence they both make the same gestures, mirror fashion: scratching head in puzzlement; shaking head; closing eyes and opening wide. Each breaks to turn to his companion; Adrienne and Humphrey are not sure which is talking to whom)

LES. [to Humphrey] Is this some   MOR. [to Adrienne] Lend me
sort of joke? Mirage? Reflec-   your pocket mirror—I'm seeing
tion from the water?   double . . .

[Adrienne and Humphrey respond appropriately, still bemused. The twins look back at each other]

LES.	*[pause]* My father's name was Peyter, and mother's Amelia.
MOR.	*[pause]* As were mine.
LES.	*[quickly]* I have a birthmark on my left shoulder.
MOR.	*[quickly]* And I on my right!
LES.	*[deliberately]* My wife's name is —Lucy!
MOR.	*[triumphant]* My wife's name is Adrienne!

[They subside, walk around each other examining thoughtfully]

LES.	Uh, I had a brother . . .
MOR.	I had a twin brother . . .
LES.	My brother was taken away . . .

MOR.	I came to California . . .
LES.	. . . and I never knew . . .
MOR.	. . . when I was a kid . . .
LES.	. . . what happened to him . . .
MOR.	. . . and never went back . . .
LES.	. . . so maybe you're maybe it's . . .
MOR.	. . . but always hoped I'd meet . . .
BOTH	BROTHER! [*They embrace. Adrienne and Humphrey are excitedly drawn into introductions, share the wonder and miracle of it all*]
LES.	[*to Adrienne*] . . . so when you told me dinner would be late, you thought I was Morley.
ADR.	[*amazed still*] Fancy that, I thought Les was Mor!
MOR.	[*to Humphrey*] . . . and when you told me we had reservations at the hotel, you thought I was Lester.
HUM.	That's right, can you imagine? I thought Mor was Les!
ADR.	[*to herself*] . . . and that tête-á-tête champagne lunch—was that Mor or Less . . . ohhhh . . .
LES.	This calls for celebrating; let's go [*gathering up the group*].
HUM.	Sure thing, Mr. S, who's springing?
MOR.	Come along, everyone, we'll split it between us, more or less.

[Exeunt]

APPENDIX A

Suggested list of rehearsal costumes and props

All of these are desirable; those marked with an asterisk are essential.

WOMEN:
* *tights
* *flat slippers; ballets will do
* *full long skirt
* *boned corselet
* *hip bolsters
  (can by made by stuffing old stockings, tying them together)
* *fan on a ribbon
* long panel, to be tied on for a train
* belt on which to hang things
* half mask, on a stick or to be worn
* shoes with 1½" heels
* head coverings

MEN:
* *tights
* *flat slippers; ballets will do
* *fitted garment to serve as doublet, jacket
* *short cape
* *sword or equivalent, with belt to wear it
* *shirt with full sleeves, cuffs
* scarf to wrap as neckcloth
* shoes with 1½" heels
* assortment of hats

BOTH:
* cloak
* walking stick
* small mirror, to wear in hat or suspended from girdle
* pomander or equivalent
* snuff box or equivalent
* gloves

APPENDIX B

Videotape (optional)

Size: VHS, Beta
Running time: 25 minutes

Two performers execute bows and curtsies; they demonstrate and dance the basic steps of the following dances:

MEDIEVAL / EARLY TUDOR	farandole
	branle
ELIZABETHAN / JACOBEAN	pavane
	galliard
RESTORATION	courante
	minuet
EIGHTEENTH CENTURY	minuet (see Restoration)
ROMANTIC	waltz
VICTORIAN / EDWARDIAN	waltz (see Romantic)
	polka

REFERENCE BIBLIOGRAPHY

Bibliographic entries were selected with the actor in mind; therefore the emphasis is on clothing, manners, background, settings, dances, weaponry, daily life, morals, culture, and recreation rather than on history or description of theatre. There is a certain amount of duplication, since various libraries will probably have different holdings, and the subject card catalog and/or computer network in each one will very likely unearth additional titles.

Titles are keyed by number to the period, as follows; the key corresponds to the chapter divisions.

1 Greek/Roman 500–100 BC
2 Medieval/Early Tudor 1200–1550
3 Elizabethan/Jacobean 1550–1640
4 Restoration 1660–1700
5 Eighteenth Century 1700–1800
6 Romantic 1780–1840
7 Victorian/Edwardian 1840–1910

A subject index follows the bibliographic entries, for quick reference to acting and period movement textbooks, clothing, dances, manners and society, theatre, and weaponry.

5   Addison, Joseph. *Selections from the Spectator Papers*. Oxford: Clarendon Press, 1907. Politics, religion, morals, manners, fashion, the stage, literature, and gossip.

1,2,3,4,   Albright, Hardie. *Acting, the Creative Process*. Belmont, CA: Dickenson Publishing Co., Inc., 1967. Acting text with period notes.
5,6,7

1   Allen, James T. *Stage Antiquities of the Greeks and Romans and Their Influence*. NY: Cooper Sq., 1963. Festivals, scenery, chorus, actors, costumes, etc.

2,3   Arbeau, Thoinet (pseud. Jehan Tabouret). *Orchesography*. NY: Dover Pubs., 1967. First pub. 1589. Dances of the 15th, 16th centuries; commentary; bibliography.

4,5,6,7   Arnold, Janet. *Patterns of Fashion*. Vol. 1: 1660–1860; Vol. 2: 1860–1940. NY: Drama Book Publishers, 1977. Englishwomen's dresses, construction, patterns.

1   Arnott, Peter D. *The Ancient Greek and Roman Theatre*. NY: Random House, 1871. Useful detail on movement, masks, acting.

2,3   Ashelford, Jane. *A Visual History of Costume: The Sixteenth Century*. NY: Drama Book Publishers, 1983.

1   Balsdon, J.P.V.D. *Roman Women: Their History and Habits*. London: Bodley Head, 1963. Divorce, drunkeness, concubinage, etc.

1   ——— . *Life and Leisure in Ancient Rome*. London: Bodley Head, 1969 and NY: McGraw Hill, 1969.

2   Barber, Richard. *The Knight and Chivalry*. London: Longman, 1970. Traditions of love, attitudes to women, tournaments, religion.

2   ——— . *The Reign of Chivalry*. Newton Abbot: David & Chure, 1980. Concept of chivalry as it affected social movements, writers, events, history.

1,2,3,4,5 Barsis, Max. *The Common Man Through the Centuries: A Book of Costume Drawings*. NY: Ungar, 1974. Sketchbook of people from the underside of history: early Greeks through the French Revolution.

1,2,3,4,   Barton, Lucy. *Historic Costume for the Stage*. Boston: Walter H. Baker Co., 1935, 1961. Drawings, description, historical setting, instructions for making, plays of the period.
5,6,7

1,2,3,4,   Batterberry, Michael & Ariane. *Mirror, Mirror: A Social History*
5,6,7   *of Fashion.* NY: Holt, Rinehart & Winston, 1977. How fashion reflects society.

7   Beeton, Mrs. Isabella. *The Book of Household Management.* London: Ward, Lock, 1981. Fac. ed. 1936, 1961, 1968. Includes domestic life in the mid-19th century.

3   Bertram, Joseph. *Acting Shakespeare.* NY: Theatre Arts Books, 1960.

4,5,6,7   Binder, Pearl. *Muffs and Morals.* NY: Wm. Morrow, 1954. Clothing and society.

2,3,4,5,   Boehn, Max von. *Modes and Manners.* Philadelphia: Lippincott,
6,7   1932–36. 7 vols. Well illustrated.

2   Bornstein, Diane. *Mirrors of Courtesy.* Hamden CT: Shoe String Press, 1975. Chivalry and social codes, rituals of courtesy.

5   Boswell, James. *Boswell's London Journal 1762–1763.* F.A. Pottle, ed. NY: McGraw Hill, 1950.

7   Bott, Alan. *Our Fathers (1870–1900)* NY: Benjamin Blom, Inc., 1972. A survey in pictures of morals, sports, war, inventions, politics.

2,3,4,5,   Bradfield, Nancy M. *Historical Costumes of England from the*
6,7   *11th to the 20th Century.* London: Harrop, 1959, 1970.

5,6,7   ——— . *Costume in Detail.* Boston: Plays, Inc., 1969, 1975. 1730–1930: designing and making women's dress.

7   Brander, Michael. *The Victorian Gentleman.* London: G. Cremonesi, 1975. Schooling, manners, morality, travel, sports, pastimes.

1,2,3,4,5, Braun, Louis, W. Diez et al. *Costumes Through the Ages.* NY:
6,7   Rizzoli, 1982. Reissue of 1850 ed. Over 1500 figures, no text.

1   Brockett, Oscar. "Producing Greek Tragedy." *Classical Journal 56, #7,* April 1961, p 322.

1   Brooke, Iris. *Costume in Greek Classical Drama.* London: Methuen and NY: Theatre Arts Books, 1962.

4,5   ——— . *Dress and Undress.* London: Methuen, 1958. Formal and informal clothing.

5,6,7   ——— . *English Children's Costume Since 1775.* London: A and C Black, 1930.

2,3,4,5,   ——— . *English Costume from the 14th Through the 19th*
6,7   *Century.* NY: Macmillan, 1937.

3 ——— . *English Costume in the Age of Elizabeth*. London: A & C Black, 1933 and NY: Barnes & Noble, 1963.

3,4 ——— . *English Costumes in the 17th Century*. London: A & C Black, 1934.

5 ——— . *English Costumes in the 18th Century*. London: A & C Black, 1934.

6,7 ——— . *English Costumes in the 19th Century*. London: A & C Black, 1934.

7 ——— . *English Costumes 1900–1950*. London: Methuen, 1951.

1,2,3,4, ——— .*Footwear: A Short History of European and Ameri-*
5,6,7 *can Shoes*. NY: Theatre Arts Books, 1972. "Shoes tell us something about people and the times they live in."

1,2,3,4, ——— . *A History of English Costume*. London: Methuen,
5,6,7 1949, 1968, 1979 and NY: Theatre Arts Books, 1972.

2 ——— . *Medieval Theatre Costume*. NY: Theatre Arts Books, 1967.

2,3, ——— . *Western European Costume I*. London: Harrap & Sons, 1940 and NY: Theatre Arts Books, 1964. Its relation to the theatre, 13th to 17th century.

4,5,6 ——— . *Western European Costume II*. London: Harrap & Sons, 1940 and NY: Theatre Arts Books, 1964. Its relation to the theatre, 17th to 19th century.

6,7 Brown, Ivor. *Dickens and his World*. London: Lutterworth Press and NY: H Z Walck, 1970.

6,7 ——— . *Dickens In his Time*. London: Thos. Nelson, 1964.

5 ——— . *Dr. Johnson and his World*. London: Lutterworth Press, 1965.

6 ——— . *Jane Austen and her World*. NY: H Z Walck, 1966. Country gentlefolk and their lives, arts and artists.

3 ——— . *Shakespeare and his World*. London: Lutterworth Press, 1964.

3 ——— . *Shakespeare in his Time*. Edinburgh: Thos. Nelson, 1960.

7 ——— . *Shaw in his Time*. London: Thos. Nelson, 1965. Attitudes toward learning, women, politics.

2   Capellanus, Andreas (André le Chapelain). *The Art of Courtly Love*. Frederick W. Locke, ed. NY: Columbia U. Press, 1941 and Ungar, 1957, 1963. Treatise on relations between sexes.

3   Casa, Giovanni della. *Galateo of Manners and Behaviours*. Boston: Marrymount Press, 1914. Written 1555. Renaissance Italian manners.

1,2,3   Cassin-Scott, Jack. *Costumes and Settings for Staging Historical Plays*.
4,7   London: Batsford and Boston: Plays Inc., 1979.

3   Castiglione, Baldassare. *The Book of the Courtier*. NY: Ungar, 1959. First pub. 1528. Tr. Friench Simpson. Philosophy and behavior of the ideal courtier.

3   Chamberlin, E.R. *Everyday Life in Renaissance Times*. NY: Capricorn Books, 1965. The Court, home, work, urban life, village life, navigation, learning.

2,3,4,5   Chisman, Isabel & Hester E. Raven-Hart. *Manners and Movements*
6,7   *in Costume Plays*. London: H F Deane and Boston: Walter H. Baker, n.d. Excellent but brief. Includes weapons, legal, processions.

3   Chute, Marchette. *Shakespeare of London*. NY: Dutton, 1949. Shakespeare in his theatre.

5,6,7   Chute, William J., ed. *The American Scene: 1600–1860*. NY: Bantam Books, 1964. Life and society: politics, Yankee character, frontier life, slavery, small town life.

1,2,3,4,   Contini, Mila. *Fashion*. James Laver, ed. NY: Odyssey Press, 1965.
5,6,7   Exceptional illustrations. Historical text includes achievements by women.

1   Cowell, F.R. *Everyday Life in Ancient Rome*. NY: Putnam's Sons, 1961. Home, school, women, clothes, food, slavery, work, professions, leisure, religion.

1,2,3,4   Crawford, Jerry L. & Joan Snyder. *Acting in Period and in Style*. Dubuque, IA: W.C. Brown, 1976. Acting text with period notes.

3,4   Cumming, Valerie. *A Visual History of Costume: The 17th Century*. NY: Drama Books, 1984.

2,3,4,5   Cunnington, Cecil W, Phillis E. Cunnington & Charles Beard. *A*
6,7   *Dictionary of English Costume 900–1900*. London: A&C Black, © 1960.

6,7   Cunnington, Cecil W. *English Women's Clothing in the 19th Century*. London: Faber & Faber, 1937, 1948.

6,7 ———— . *Feminine Attitudes in the 19th Century.* NY: Haskel House, 1935, 1973. History, condition of women, social life, fashion.

2,3 Cunnington, Cecil W. & Phillis Cunnington. *Handbook of English Costume in the 16th Century.* Boston: Plays Inc., 1972 rev.

3,4 ———— . *Handbook of English Costume in the 17th Century.* London: Faber & Faber, 1955, 1967.

5 ———— . *Handbook of English Costume in the 18th Century.* London: Faber & Faber. 1957 and Boston: Plays Inc. 1972.

6,7 ———— . *Handbook of English Costume in the 19th Century.* London: Faber & Faber, 1959, 1973.

2 ———— . *Handbook of English Medieval Costume.* London: Faber & Faber, 1952, rev. 1969.

2,3,4,5 ———— . *A Picture History of English Costume.* London: Vista Books,
6,7 1960.

2,3,4,5 ———— . *The History of Underclothes.* London: Faber & Faber, 1981
6,7 rev. First pub. 1951.

2,3,4,5 Cunnington, Phillis E. *Costume in Pictures.* NY: Dutton Picture-
6,7 back, 1964.

2,3,4,5 Cunnington, Phillis & Catherine Lucas. *Occupational Costume in*
6,7 *England from the 11th Century to 1914.* NY: Barnes & Noble, 1967.

2,3,4,5 Cunnington, Phillis E. *Costume of Household Servants, From Middle*
6,7 *Ages to 1900.* NY: Barnes & Noble, 1975.

2,3,4,5 Cunnington, Phillis E. & Alan Mansfield. *English Costumes for*
6,7 *Sports and Outdoor Recreation from the 16th to 19th Centuries.* London: A & C Black, 1969.

7 ———— . *Handbook of English Costume in the 20th Century.* Boston: Plays Inc., 1973.

1 Davis, Wm. Stearns. *A Day in Old Athens.* Boston: Allyn & Bacon, 1914. Home, street life, market, military, children, customs, politics, religion, festivals, slavery, etc.

1 ———— . *A Day in Old Rome.* Boston: Allyn & Bacon, 1925. Home, street life, market, military, children, customs, politics, religion, festivals, slavery, etc.

2 ———— . *Life in a Medieval Barony.* NY: Harper & Bros., 1923. Picture of a typical feudal community in the 13th century.

3 ———. *Life in Elizabethan Days*. NY: Harper & Bros., 1930. Picture of a typical English community at the end of the 16th century.

3,4 De Lauze, F. *Apologie de la Danse*. London: Frederick Muller, 1952. First pub. 1623. In English and French. Treatise of instruction in dancing and deportment; salutations, dances.

7 Delgado, Alan. *Victorian Entertainments*. NY: American Heritage Press, 1971.

3,4,5,6, DeMarly, Diana. *Costumes on the Stage 1600–1940*. Totowa, NJ:
7 Barnes & Noble, 1982.

3 Dodd, Arthur Herbert. *Life in Elizabethan England*. London: Batsford, 1961.

2,3 Dolmetsch, Mabel. *Dances of England and France from 1450 to 1600*. London: Routledge & Paul, 1949 and NY: Da Capo, 1975. Dance directions can be followed.

2,3 ———. *Dances of Italy and Spain from 1400–1600*. London: Routledge & Paul, 1954 and NY: Da Capo, 1975. Dance directions can be followed.

1,2,3,4, Durant, Will & Ariel. *The Story of Civilization*. 10 vols. NY: Simon
5 & Schuster, 1937–67. Contains segments on life, manners, morals, beliefs, theatre.

3 Edelen, Georges, ed. *The Description of England*. Ithaca: Cornell U. Press, 1968. Shakespeare's England.

3,4 Erlanger, Philippe. *The Age of Courts and Kings, 1558–1715*. NY: Harper & Row, 1967. Manners and morals.

5 Essex, John. *The Young Ladies Conduct*. London: J. Brotherton, 1722. Rules for education, on dress, advice to young wives.

1,2,3,4, Ewing, Elizabeth. *Dress and Undress: A History of Women's Under-*
5,6,7 *wear*. NY: Drama Books, 1978.

1,2,3,4 ———. *Underwear, A History*. NY: Theatre Arts Books, 1972.
5,6,7

2,3,4,5 Fernald, Mary & Eileen Shenton. *Costume Design and Making*. NY:
6,7 Theatre Arts Books, 1967 and London: A & C Black, 1937, 1957.

1 Flaceliere, Robert. *Daily Life in Greece at the Time of Pericles*. Tr. Peter Green. London: Widenfeld & Nicolson, 1965.

7 Foster, Vanda & Christina Walkley. *Crinoline and Crimping Irons: Victorian Clothes, How They Were Cleaned and Cared For*. London: Owen, 1978.

146

6,7   Foster, Vanda. *A Visual History of Costume: The Nineteenth Century.* NY: Drama Books, 1984.

7   Gernsheim, Alison. *Victorian and Edwardian Fashion: A Photographic Survey.* NY: Dover, ©1981. Originally pub. as *Fashion and Reality (1840–1914)*. London: Faber & Faber, 1963.

2   Gies, Joseph & Frances Gies. *Life in a Medieval City.* NY: Crowell, 1969. Northwest Europe in the 12th and 13th centuries; life, death, business, recreation, town fairs, government.

7   Gilmour, Robin. *The Idea of the Gentleman in the Victorian Novel.* London & Boston: Allen & Unwin, 1981. Literary criticism and social history.

2,3,4,5,   Girouard, Mark. *Life in the English Country House.* New Haven: Yale
6,7   U. Press, 1978. A "social and architectural history;" customs of daily life.

6,7   ——— . *The Return to Camelot: Chivalry and the English Gentleman.* New Haven: Yale U. Press, 1981. Revival of chivalry in the 19th century to World War I.

3,4   Glenn, Stanley L. *The Complete Actor.* Boston: Allyn & Bacon, 1977. Acting text with period notes.

1,2,3,4,   Gorsline, Douglas W. *What People Wore.* NY: Viking Press, 1952.
5,6,7   Visual history of dress from antiquity to 20th century America.

1,2,3,4,   Green, Ruth M. *The Wearing of Costume.* London: Pitman, 1966.
5,6,7   Clothes and how to move in them.

1   Gulick, Charles Burton. *The Life of the Ancient Greeks.* NY: Cooper Sq. Pub., 1973 reprint of 1902 ed. Growing up, occupations, marriage, home, clothing, social life, professions, travel.

1,2,3,4   Hansen, Henny H. *Costumes and Styles.* NY: Dutton, 1956.
5,6

1,3,4,5,   Harrop, John & Sabin R. Epstein. *Acting With Style.* Englewood
6,7   Cliffs, NJ: Prentice-Hall, 1982.

2   Hart, Roger. *English Life in Chaucer's Day.* NY: Putnam, 1973.

3,4   ——— . *English Life in the 17th Century.* NY: Putnam, 1971.

5   ——— . *English Life in the 18th Century.* NY: Putnam, 1970.

2,3   ——— . *English Life in Tudor Times.* London: Wayland and NY: Putnam, 1972.

2,3,4,5 Hartley, Dorothy & Margaret Elliot. *Life and Work of the People of England*. London: Batsford, 1926–31 6 vols. 11th through 18th century.

2 Hartley, Dorothy. *Medieval Costume and Life*. NY: Scribners and London: Batsford, 1931.

4 Henshaw, N. Wandalee. "Graphic Sources for a Modern Approach to the Acting of Restoration Comedy." *Educational Theatre J.* XX-2, May 1968. Includes rehearsal techniques applicable to all periods.

2,3,4,5, Hill, Margot Hamilton & Peter A. Bucknell. *The Evolution of Fash-*
6,7 *ion: Pattern and Cut From 1066 to 1930*. NY: Drama Books, 1977. First pub. 1964. Includes scale patterns.

4,5 Hilton, Wendy. *Dance of Court and Theater: The French Noble Style 1690–1725*. Princeton, NJ: Princeton Book Co., 1981. Includes Court etiquette, bows, curtsies.

2,3,4,5, Hobbs, William. *Stage Combat, "The Action to the Word."* London:
6,7 Barrie & Jenkins, 1980.

2,3,4,5 ———. *Stage Fight*. NY: Theatre Arts Books, 1967. Swords, fire-
6,7 arms, fisticuffs, slapstick.

3,4,5,6, Hole, Christina. *British Folk Customs*. London: Hutchinson, 1976.
7

2,3,4,5, ———. *English Custom and Usage*. London and NY: Batsford,
6,7 1950. 3rd ed.

2,3,4,5 ———. *English Homelife 1500–1800*. London: Batsford, 1949.

3,4 ———. *The English Housewife in the 17th Century*. London: Chatto & Windus, 1953.

3,4,5,6 ———. *English Sports and Pastimes*. London: Batsford, 1949.

3,4,5,6, ———. *English Traditional Customs*. Totowa, NJ: Rowman & Lit-
7 tlefield, 1975.

1 Hope, Thomas. *Costumes of the Greeks and Romans*. NY: Dover, 1962.

2,3 Horst, Louis. *Pre-Classic Dance Forms*. NY: Kamin, 1953 and Brooklyn: Dance Horizons, 1968, reprint of 1937 ed. History and description; dances not easy to reproduce.

7 Hughes, Molly V. *A Victorian Family*. London: Oxford U. Press, 1978. 3 vols. Details of everyday life in London.

5   Jarrett, Derek. *England in the Age of Hogarth.* London: Hart-Davis, MacGibbon and NY: Viking, 1974. Life in 18th century England.

2,3,4,5,   Johnson, Reginald Brunley, ed. *Manners Makyth Man.* London:
6,7   A.M. Philpot, 1927. Anthology of great writers illustrating manners and customs, Chaucer through 19th century.

6,7   Johnston, Wm. McAllister. *Vienna, Vienna: The Golden Age 1815–1914.* NY: Potter, 1981. City of waltzes, operettas, Beethoven, Schubert, Mahler, Freud.

2,3,4,5   Kelly, Francis Michael & Randolph Schwabe. *Historic Costume, A Chronicle of Fashion in Western Europe, 1490–1790.* NY: Scribner's, 1925 and NY: Blom, 1968.

2,3,4,5   ——— . *A Short History of Costume and Armour, Chiefly in England 1066–1800.* London: Batsford, 1931 and NY: Arco, 1972.

3   Kelly, Francis Michael. *Shakespearian Costume for Stage and Screen.* London: A.C. Black, 1938. 2nd ed. 1970, rev. by Alan Mansfield.

1   Kernodle, George. "Symbolic Action in the Greek Choral Odes." *Classical J.* 53 (Oct. 1957). Variety of visual choral functions.

2,3,4,5,   Keyes, Jean. *A History of Women's Hairstyles, 1500–1965.* London:
6,7   Methuen, 1967.

1   King, Anthony. *Archaeology of Ancient Rome.* NY: Crescent Books, 1981. Daily life interpreted from ruins: attitudes to animals, marriage, army: technology, trade, leisure, entertainment, myth, religion, visual arts.

6,7   ——— . *Buildings and Society.* London: Routledge & Kegan Paul, 1980. Essays on the social development of the built environment.

2   Koch, H.W. *Medieval Warfare.* London: Bison Books, 1978. Warfare, armor, equipment, seige technique, castles, fortifications.

7   Lasdun, Susan. *Victorians at Home.* NY: Viking, 1981.

5,6   Laver, James. *The Age of Illusion: Manners and Morals 1750–1848.* NY: D. McKay and London: Weidenfeld & Nicolson, 1972. England and France.

1,2,3,4   ——— . *Concise History of Costume and Fashion.* NY: H.M.
5,6,7   Abrams, 1969 and NY: Oxford U. Press, 1983 (rev. title *A Concise History*)

1,2,3,4   ——— . *Costume.* London: Batsford, 1956 and London: Cassell,
5,6,7   1963 and NY: Hawthorn Books, 1964.

1 ———. *Costume in Antiquity*. NY: C. N. Potter, 1964.

1,2,3,4 ———. *Costume Through the Ages, 1000 Illustrations*. NY: Simon
5,6,7 & Schuster, 1963.

7 ———. *Edwardian Promenade*. Boston: Houghton Mifflin, 1958.
Social life and customs.

7 ———. *Manners and Morals in the Age of Optimism, 1848–1914*.
NY: Harper & Row, 1966. English ed.: *The Age of Optimism: Manners and Morals 1848–1914*. London: Weidenfeld & Nicolson,
1966. England, France.

6,7 ———. *Taste and Fashion*. London: Harrap, 1946.

7 ———. *Victorian Vista: Social Life and Customs*. London: Hulton
Press, 1954.

1 Lawler, Lillian. *Dance in Ancient Greece*. London: A. C. Black,
1964. Also pub. as *The Dance of the Ancient Greek Theatre*. Iowa
City: U. of Iowa Press, 1964. Detailed description of choral
movements.

2,3,4,5 Lawson, Joan. *European Folk Dance*. London: Pitman, 1953.
6,7 National and musical characteristics; examples of steps.

3 Lee, Jr., Maurice. *Dudley Carleton to John Chamberlain: 1603–1624
Jacobean Letters*. New Brunswick: Rutgers U., 1972. Masquerades
and theatricals which delighted the nobility.

4,5,6,7 Lejeune, Anthony. *The Gentlemen's Clubs of London*. NY: May-
flower Books, 1979. Their significant role in the social and political
history of Britain.

7 Levine, George, ed. *The Emergence of Victorian Consciousness, The
Spirit of the Age*. NY: Free Press, 1967.

3,4,5 Levron, Jaques. *Daily Life at Versailles in the 17th–18th Centuries*. Tr.
Claire Eliane Engel. London: Allen & Unwin, 1968.

4 Lewis, Warren Hamilton. *The Splendid Century*. NY: Doubleday &
Co., 1957. Especially the chapter "The Art of Living."

2,3,4,5, Lister, Margot. *Costumes of Everyday Life*. Boston: Plays Inc., 1972.
6,7 History of working clothes in Europe, 900–1910.

1,2,3,4, ———. *Costume: An Illustrated Survey from Ancient Times to the
5,6,7 20th Century*. Boston Plays, Inc., 1968, 1971. Includes hair styles,
ecclesiastical, naval, military dress in Spain, Italy, Germany,
Netherlands.

1,2,3,4   Lord, W. B. *The Corset and the Crinoline.* London: Ward, Lock & Tyler, 1868. Modes and costumes.

7   Macqueen-Pope, Walter James. *Twenty Shillings in the Pound.* London & NY: Hutchinson, 1949. Middle-class English social life and customs, 1890–1914.

4,5,6,7   Mansfield, Alan. *Ceremonial Costume: Court, Civil and Civic Costume from 1660 to the Present Day.* London: Black, 1980. England.

3,4,5   Marks, Marcia. "This is the Dance That Was." *Dance Magazine 41* (July 1967), pp 44–48. Choreographer William Burdick on period customs and dances.

3,4,5   Mason, John E. *Gentlefolk in the Making: Studies in the History of English Courtesy Literature, Etc.* Philadelphia: Philadelphia U. Press, 1935. List of anthologies and secondary studies on etiquette, social life, and customs, 1531–1774.

2,3,4,5,   Mason, Philip. *The English Gentleman: The Rise and Fall of an Ideal.*
6,7   London: Andre Deutsch, 1982. Social status and moral attributes, Chaucer to modern day.

7   Mayhew, Henry. *German Life and Manners, 1864.* London: W. H. Allen, 1864. Village, town, fashionable, domestic, married, school, and university life, etc.

7   ———— . *London's Underworld.* Peter Quennell, ed. London: Spring Books, 1958. Victorian outcasts of society, and attitudes toward them.

1   McDaniel, Walton Brooks. *Roman Private Life and its Survivals.* NY: Cooper Sq., 1963. Home, childhood, clothing, gods, daily life, social life, amusements, travel, street life.

3   Meader, William G. *Courtship in Shakespeare.* NY: Columbia U. Press, 1954. Love and courtship in the plays.

3   Mehl, Dieter. *The Elizabethan Dumb Show.* London: Methuen, 1965.

2,3,4,5,   Muir, Richard. *The English Village.* NY: Thomas & Hudson, 1980.
6,7   Customs and settings, from primitive origins to the 20th century.

3   Nicoll, Allardyce. *The Elizabethans.* Cambridge: Cambridge U. Press, 1957. Annotated quotations, 1558 to 1603, on government, church, London, recreation, countryside, home, school, travel, science, art, military.

5   Nivelon, F. *The Rudiments of Genteel Behavior.* Pub. 1737. Manners, salutations, how to dance the minuet.

2,3,4,5,   Oxenford, Lyn. *Playing Period Plays.* Chicago: Coach House Press,
6,7   1957. Valuable; broad range; includes lists of useful books, plays of the period. Dances not easy to reproduce.

1,2,3,4   Palffy-Alper, Julius. *Sword and Masque.* Philadelphia: F.A. Davis Co., 1967. Fencing description and instruction. Section on theatrical fencing includes other weapons and exercises.

7   *Patterns of History: A Series of 8 Individual Patterns.* NY: Drama Books, 1979. Women's clothing, housedress to dinner gown and a bicycling suit. Construction guide. Drawings of hair, hats, and wraps.

3   Pearson, Lu Emily. *Elizabethans At Home.* Stanford, CA: Stanford U. Press, 1957.

4   Pepys, Samuel. *Diary and Correspondence.* NY: Bigelow Brown & Co., n.d. 4 vols. Diary 1660–1669.

7   Perugini, Mark. *Victorian Days and Ways.* London: Hutchinson & Co., 1932? Amusements, streets, youth, life of classes, fashions, theatre, arts.

1   Pickard-Cambridge, A.W. *The Dramatic Festivals of Athens.* Oxford: Oxford U. Press, 1953.

3   Playford, John. *Court Dances and Others.* London: J. Curwen, 1911. Pavane, Galliard, others.

3   ——— . *English Dancing Master.* London: Hugh Mellor, 1933. First pub. 1651. Primary source for country dances: rounds, longways, squares, etc. with music.

6   Plumb, John Harold. *Georgian Delights.* Boston: Little Brown, 1980. Life in Georgian England.

5   Porter, Roy. *English Society in the 18th Century.* London: Allen Lane, 1982.

1   Prescott, Henry W. "Silent Roles in Roman Comedy." *Classical Philology XXXI, #2,* April 1936, pp 97–119. Actions of supernumeraries.

1,2,3,4,   Prisk, Berneice & Jack A. Byers. *Theatre Student Costuming.* NY:
5,6,7   Richards Rosen Press, 1970. For making basic rehearsal costume parts added to tights and leotard.

1,2   Quennell, Marjorie & C.H.B. *Everyday Life in Roman and Anglo-Saxon Times.* NY: Putnam's Sons, 1927 and rev. ed. London: Batsford, 1959. Includes Viking and Norman periods.

1   ————. *Everyday Things in Ancient Greece.* NY: Putnam's Sons, 1954, 1957.

2,3,4,5, ————. *A History of Everyday Things in England.* 4 vols. London:
6,7   Batsford, 1954–58.

5,6,7 Quennell, Peter, ed. *Affairs of the Mind: The Salon in Europe and America from the 18th to the 20th Century.* Washington DC: New Republic Books, 1980. High society.

7   ————. *The Day Before Yesterday.* London: J.M. Dent, 1978. Photographic album of daily life in Victorian/Edwardian Britain.

6,7   ————. *Genius in the Drawing Room: The Literary Salon in the 19th and 20th Centuries.* London: Wiedenfeld & Nicolson, 1980. Exchange of ideas.

7   ————. *Victorian Panorama.* London: Batsford, 1937. Life and fashion from contemporary photographs.

5   Rameau, Pierre. *The Dancing Master.* Cyril Beaumont, tr. of *Maitre à Danser*, Paris 1725. London: C.W. Beaumont, 1941. Comportment, salutations, Court etiquette, Court dances.

5   Ribeiro, Aileen. *A Visual History of Costume: The Eighteenth Century.* NY: Drama Books, 1983.

6,7   Richardson, Philip J.S. *The Social Dances of the Nineteenth Century in England.* London: H. Jenkins, 1960. Traces development of social dances.

2,3,4,5 Rockwood, Jerome. *The Craftsmen of Dionysus.* Glenview, IL: Scott
6,7   Foresman, 1966. Acting text with period notes.

2   Rowling, Marjorie. *Everyday Life in Medieval Times.* NY: Putnam, 1968. Classes, townsfolk, traders, women and wives, schools, ecclesiastics, etc.

3   Rowse, A.L. *Sex and Society in Shakespeare's Age: Simon Forman the Astrologer.* NY: Scribner, 1974. Private life in Elizabethan England.

1,2,3,4, Russell, Douglas. *Period Style for the Theatre.* Boston: Allyn &
5,6,7 Bacon, 1980. Art, culture, ideals, clothing, manners, plays.

1,2,3,4, ————. *Theatrical Style, A Visual Approach to the Theatre.* Palo
5,6,7 Alto, CA: Mayfield, 1976.

2,3,4,5, Russell, Elizabeth. *Adaptable Stage Costume for Women.* London:
6,7   Miller, 1974. 100 costumes in one.

3,4   Sabol, Andrew J., ed. *Four Hundred Songs and Dances from the Stuart Masque*. Providence: Brown U. Press, 1978. Enlarged ed. of his *Songs and Dances for the Stuart Masque*, 1959.

1,2,3,4,   Sachs, Curt. *The Commonwealth of Art*. NY: W. W. Norton, 1946.
5,6,7   The arts of a time reflect the prevailing images and themes.

1,2,3,4,   ———— . *World History of the Dance*. NY: W. W. Norton, 1937.
5,6,7   Chapter 7, "Europe Since Antiquity," dances from ancient Greece to 1900.

7   Sackville-West, Vita. *The Edwardians*. Garden City, NY: Double-day Doran, 1930. Chronicle of the last years of a decorative aristocracy.

3   Salgado, Ramway G.N. *The Elizabethan Underworld*. London: Dent and Totowa, NJ: Rowman & Littlefield, 1977. Tinkers, peddlers, jugglers, whores, card shapes, fortune tellers.

2   Salzman, L.F. *England in Tudor Times*. London: Batsford, 1926. Social life in towns, country, home; the spirit of the age.

3   Schoenbaum, Samuel. *Shakespeare: The Globe and the World*. NY: Oxford U. Press, 1979. Chapter 2, "The London Years" on customs, costumes, society.

5   Scott, Arthur Finley. *The Early Hanoverian Age 1714–1760*. London: Croom Helm, 1980. Commentaries on an era.

5,6   ———— . *Every One a Witness: The Georgian Age*. London: Martins, 1970. Social life and customs.

2   ———— . *Every One a Witness: The Norman Age*. London: White Lion, 1976. Social life and customs.

2   ———— . *Every One a Witness: The Plantagenet Age*. London: and NY: White Lion, 1975. Social life and customs.

1,2   ———— . *Every One a Witness: The Saxon Age*. London: Croom Helm, 1979. Social life and customs.

3,4,5   ———— . *Every One a Witness: The Stuart Age*. London: White Lion, 1974. Social life and customs.

2,3   ———— . *Every One a Witness: The Tudor Age*. London: White Lion, 1975. Social life and customs.

1,2,3,4   Selbie, R. *The Anatomy of Costume*. NY: Crescent Books, 1977.
5,6,7

3,4,5,6   Seyler, Athene. "Fans, Trains and Stays." *Theatre Arts 31* (Novem-
7   ber 1947), pp 21–24. How to approach work in period costumes.

1,2,3,4, Sichel, Marion. *Costume Reference.* Boston: Plays Inc., 1977–78. 8
5,6,7   vols.

2,3,4,5   Sorell, Walter. *Dance In Its Time.* NY: Anchor Press/Doubleday,
6,7   1981. How the arts are integrated with the philosophy, conduct,
          and ideals of the time.

3,4,5,6, Squire, Geoffrey. *Dress and Society.* NY: Viking, 1974. Orig. pub. as
7   *Dress, Art and Society 1560–1970.*

5   Stanhope, Philip Donner (4th Earl of Chesterfield). *The Letters of
          the Earl of Chesterfield to His Son.* London: Methuen, 1901. 2 vols.
          Advice on conduct and behavior, 1774.

1,2,3,4, Strutt, Joseph. *The Sports and Pastimes of the People of England.*
5   London: Methuen, 1903. First pub. 1796.

7   Sutherland, Douglas. *The English Gentelmen's Wife.* London:
          Debrett's Peerage, 1979. The English Lady, invented by Queen
          Victoria. Marriage, social life, and customs.

1   Taplin, Oliver. *Greek Tragedy in Action.* Berkeley & Los Angeles:
          U. of California Press, 1978. Visual techniques of communication,
          movement, stance, space, etc.

2,3,4,5   Taylor, Lou. *Mourning Dress.* London: Allyn & Unwin, 1983. Cos-
6,7   tume and social history, etiquette.

1,2,3,4, Tegg, William. *The Knot Tied.* Detroit: Swinging Tree Press, 1970
5,6,7   (fac. ed.). First pub. 1877. Marriage customs of all nations.

1,2,3,4, ————. *The Last Act.* Detroit: Gale Research, 1973. First pub.
5,6,7   1876. Funeral rites of nations and individuals.

3,4   Thompson, Roger, ed. *Samuel Pepys' Penny Merriments.* NY:
          Columbia U. Press, 1977. Aspirations, wit, prejudices, jests, magic,
          amorous tales, rogues, fools, 17th century.

7   Tickell, Jerrard. *Gentlewomen Aim to Please.* London: Routledge,
          1938. Gentlemen too; Victorian manners, dress, dining, ballroom,
          courtship, matrimony.

1,2,3,4, Traill, H. D. & J. S. Mann, eds. *Social England.* London: Cassell,
5,6,7   1894–1904. 6 vols. Religion, law, learning, arts, industry, com-
          merce, science, manners.

4,5   Trotti de La Chétardie, Jacques Joachim. *Instructions For a Young Nobleman*. London: R. Bentley & S. Magnes, 1683. "The idea of a person of honour in daily life, in the Court, how to write; Christian & Moral Maxims."

5   Turberville, A. S. *English Men and Manners of the 18th Century*. NY: Oxford U. Press, 1957. First pub. 1926.

5   ——— . *Johnson's England*. Oxford: Clarendon Press, 1933, 1952. English life and manners.

4,5,6,7   Turner, E. S. *The History of Courting*. London & NY: Dutton, 1955.

1,2,3,4, 5,6,7   Urian, Dan. "The Meaning of Costume." Monograph. Oakland, CA: Personabooks, 1984. How costume reveals social and economic status, age, relationships, character.

2,3,4,5, 6,7   Waugh, Nora. *Corsets and Crinolines*. London: Batsford, 1954. Includes construction notes.

3,4,5,6, 7   ——— . *The Cut of Men's Clothes, 1600–1900*. London: Faber, 1964. Includes cutting diagrams and patterns.

3,4,5,6, 7   ——— . *The Cut of Women's Clothes, 1600–1930*. London: Faber, 1968. Includes cutting diagrams and patterns.

1   Webster, T. B. L. *The Greek Chorus*. London: Methuen, 1970.

7   West, Rebecca. *1900*. London: Weidenfeld & Nicolson, 1982. Events, painters, writers, politics, scientists, composers, drama, philosophy.

2   Whitmore, Mary Elizabeth. *Medieval English Domestic Life and Amusements in the Works of Chaucer*. Washington DC: The Catholic University of America, 1937. Houses, gardens, meals, table manners, dress, sports, pastimes.

2,3,4,5, 6,7   Wildeblood, Joan & Peter Brinson. *The Polite World*. London: Oxford U. Press, 1965 and rev. ed. London: David-Poynter, 1973. Highly detailed on English manners, 13th–19th centuries. Rev. ed. omits four chapters, adds 20th century pre-war and post-war.

3   Williams, John T. *Costumes and Settings for Shakespeare's Plays*. Totowa NJ: Barnes & Noble, 1982.

1,2,3,4, 5,6,7   Williams-Mitchell, Christobel. *Dressed for the Job: The Story of Occupational Costume*. NY: Sterling, 1982. English history, work, work clothes, laboring classes.

3   Wilson, John Dover. *Life in Shakespeare's England*. London: Penguin, 1964.

1,2,3,4,   Wise, Arthur. *Weapons in the Theatre*. London: Longmans, 1968.
5   For director and actor, how to handle scenes of violence; stage, film, TV.

4   Wood, Melusine. *Advanced Historical Dances*. London: Imperial Society/C. W. Beaumont, 1960. Minuet, contredanse.

2,3,4,5   ——— . *Historical Dances from the 12th to the 19th Century*. London: Imperial Society/C. W. Beaumont, 1964. Branle, pavane, estampie, basse dance, galliard, minuet, allemande.

2,3,4   ——— . *More Historical Dances*. London: Imperial Society/C. W. Beaumont, 1966. Pavane, corrente, minuet; deportment, salutations.

2,3,4,5,   Yarwood, Doreen. *Costume of the Western World*. NY: St. Martin's,
6,7   1980c.

1,2,3,4,   ——— . *English Costume From the 2nd Century BC to 1960*. London:
5,6,7   Batsford, 1967. First pub. 1952 (. . . *to 1950*).

1,2,3,4,   ——— . *European Costume: 4000 Years of Fashion*. London: Bats-
5,6,7   ford & NY: Larousse, 1975.

7   Young, G. M. *Victorian England*. London: Oxford U. Press, 1936, 1937, 1953, 1961, 1977. Portrait of an age.

1,2,3,4,   Young, Stark. "Wearing Costumes." *Theatre Practice*. NY: Scribner,
5,6,7   1926. Also in *Theatre*, Edith J. F. Isaacs, ed. Boston: Little, Brown, 1927. Costume and its culture; costume must be carried and animated—the actor fulfills the image.

SUBJECT INDEX FOR BIBLIOGRAPHY

In this subject index, authors are listed under the following categories (figures in parentheses indicate the number of titles):

> Acting texts; period movement texts
> Costumes; some include patterns
> Dances
> Manners, customs, society
> Theatre
> Weaponry
> Masks: see pp 20–21

ACTING TEXTS; PERIOD MOVEMENT TEXTS

Albright	Crawford	Lawler
Bertram	Glenn	Oxenford
Brockett	Harrop	Rockwood
Chisman	Henshaw	

COSTUMES

Arnold	Ewing (2)	PATTERNS . . .
Ashelford	Fernald	Prisk
Barsis	Foster (2)	Ribeiro
Barton	Gernsheim	Russell, E.
Batterberry	Gorsline	Selbie
Binder	Green	Seyler
Bradfield (2)	Hansen	Sichel
Braun	Hill	Squire
Brooke (14)	Hope	Taylor
Cassin-Scott	Kelly (3)	Urian
Contini	Keyes	Waugh (3)
Cumming	Laver (5)	Williams
Cunnington, C. (9)	Lister (2)	Williams-Mitchell
Cunnington, P. (5)	Lord	Yarwood
DeMarly	Mansfield	Young, S.

DANCES

Arbeau	Lawler	Rameau
De Lauze	Lawson	Richardson
Dolmetsch (2)	Marks	Sachs
Hilton	Nivelon	Wood (3)
Horst	Playford (2)	

MANNERS, CUSTOMS, SOCIETY

Addison	Gulick	Porter
Balsdon (2)	Harrop	Quennell, M. (3)
Barber (2)	Hart (4)	Quennell, P. (4)
Batterberry	Hartley (2)	Rowling
Beeton	Hilton	Rowse
Binder	Hole (6)	Russell, D.
Boehn	Hughes	Sachs
Bornstein	Jarrett	Sackville-West
Boswell	Johnson	Salgado
Bott	Johnston	Salzman
Brander	King (2)	Schoenbaum
Brown, I. (7)	Lasdun	Scott (7)
Capellanus	Laver (4)	Sorell
Casa	Lee	Squire
Castiglione	Lejeune	Stanhope
Chamberlin	Levine	Strutt
Chisman	Levron	Sutherland
Chute	Lewis	Taylor
Cowell	Macqueen-Pope	Tegg (2)
Cunnington, C.	Marks	Thompson
Davis (4)	Mason, J.	Tickell
Delgado	Mason, P.	Traill
Dodd	Mayhew (2)	Trotti de
Durant	McDaniel	La Chétardie
Edelen	Muir	Turberville (2)
Erlanger	Nicoll	Turner
Essex	Nivelon	West
Flaceliere	Pearson	Whitmore
Gies	Pepys	Wildeblood
Gilmour	Perugini	Wilson
Girouard (2)	Plumb	Young, G.M.

159

THEATRE

Allen	Meader	Russell, D.
Arnott	Mehl	Sabol
Chute	Pickard-Cambridge	Taplin
Kernodle	Prescott	Webster

WEAPONRY

Hobbs (2)
Koch
Palffy-Alper
Wise